Kaleidoscope

Kaleidoscope

Making the Necessary Adjustments to See Yourself As God Sees You

Andrea Bing Brown

Kaleidoscope

Published by:
Professional Woman Publishing
www.pwnbooks.com

ISBN: 978-0-578-14227-2

Lauren A. Brown, Illustrator and Graphic Designer
Tara Maldonaldo, Photographer

Contents

Dedication

As a first-time writer, I find this section humbling because each entry in my book is due in large part to those mentioned below. They sacrificed their time, talent and treasure to make my dreams come true. I am forever indebted to them and pray the Lord would continue to bless their lives.

I first want to thank my mother, the late Ethel Audrey Bing. You inspired me to write this book for all the little girls and families who struggle with the loss of a parent and the self-defeating thoughts that go along with such a loss when it goes unchecked. You instilled in me, for those seven years of my life, a love for family, God's people and myself. When you passed away, you left your kind heart, spirit and love with me. The love you had for Tony and me, was passed down to my children and grandchildren. Even though your loss is sorely missed today, I know your spirit will live in me forever. I love you mommy.

I am thankful to my father, William N. Bing a.k.a. "My Stalker Daddy." I have said this to you in private but a public proclamation is in order. Our relationship is an example of what God can do when you have a father who was persistent in restoring a relationship with his daughter that was strained due to life's mishaps. You taught me about restoration, self-forgiveness, and a love for family despite their flaws. You are the Bing Family's patriarch and I'm so honored to call you my Daddy. I'm so thankful to God for restoring our love and respect for one another. I love you daddy.

To my five feet mom, the late Virginia Mance. You epitomized truth, love and respect of self for Tony and me to model. I couldn't imagine raising my grandkids as a single parent. But you dug your heels in deep, relied on the Lord for strength and slapped us when we got out of hand. I never knew how much you were my rock until your passing. I miss our dozens of conversations during the course of the day about nothing in particular. You were my best friend and loved me unconditionally. You spent your years helping to raise my children who adored your stories about things I forbade you telling them. Life without you has been lonely but I thank you for leaving me your example of persevering through difficult times and to never stop praising the Lord despite the pain. Mommy and I are proud of how you raised Tony and me. Rest on my hero! Rest on!

To Anisha, Reggie Jr., Colleen and Lauren, my children, my joy and loves of my life. Thank you for allowing me to practice patience, forgiveness and love on the four of you. You have taught me how to appreciate my blessings of having children who are good natured, with an awesome work ethic and have a love for one another. You make every day of my life special, full of goodness and good times particularly with the grandchildren. You guys are pure love and the Lord's truest gifts to me. I love you so much.

To my dear brother, Anthony E. Bing. We have been through a lot but we are still here fighting the good fight of faith. Thank you for the many laughs and arguments during our childhood. You made life interesting and worth living. I love you big brother!

To Kia Aileen Bing-Davies a.k.a. "Kiki" my baby sister. Thank you for planting in my spirit the idea of writing a book back in 2009, while sharing one of our warm sisterly conversations via Skype. I pray that the Lord would continue to bless us with plenty of times to bask in our geniuses over future endeavors to come. I love brainstorming with you.

To Enette Vaden Johnson, my prayer partner of 11 years. You are my Proverbs 27:17 friend. We have cried, laughed, argued, studied and prayed together and I am honored to call you my friend, my sister. You never shied away from telling me the truth even to the point of risking our friendship. We are kindred souls to the point that we both can sense when something is not quite right with each other. Thank you for praying with me, holding my confidences and loving me through the tough times. You're still my pain! I love you E!

To Rev. Niki Brown, my mentor, my counselor, my friend. Thank you for speaking into my life in 2004 when my former life blew up in my face. All that was lost brought great distress to my mind and soul. Your counseling and love for spiritual wholeness was the foundation you laid for my healing. You walked me step by step through the tears, stubbornness and realization that life will get better. You understand what it takes to be free from self-defeat and I'm eternally grateful for your guidance. The seeds you planted and continue to plant are finally manifesting a harvest of joy and direction. You are greatly admired and I love you.

To Bishop David G. Evans, my Pastor. My first encounter with you was one month after I joined Bethany in 2003. I couldn't believe as large as our church is, you actually found the time within a few hours to return my call. I appreciate your guidance, direction and love for what's true in the Lord. You speak the truth with passion and love and it is evident in my life. I didn't believe in being 'slain in the spirit' until you laid hands on me during a healing service in 2011. When I got up off the floor and found my way back to my seat, I looked at you and thought with confusion "what did you just do to me." That never happened to me before and I knew then that the power of the Lord was upon you. Thank you for the many times you counseled me out of making many poor choices that changed the direction of my future. You are teaching me the value of being a consistent, dedicated Christian and stress the importance of appreciating the grace, mercy and love of God concerning me. Thank you for your dedication, love and patience. I love you Bishop.

To my core inner circle of family, adopted mothers and friends; you know who you are. You have walked this path with me encouraging and praying for me along the way. Your words of encouragement and gifts during difficult times blessed me abundantly. I am here today because of your influence, and I appreciate your love of sacrifice.

I would like to thank Linda Ellis Eastman and The Professional Woman Network for cultivating my passion for self-expression. Thank you for helping me launch my message to the world.

To my Lord and Savior Jesus Christ. Your words in Psalm 139:13-14 state that you created me and knit me together in my mother's womb. I am fearfully and wonderfully made. You created me for this life, this day, this moment. You knew it was necessary for me to go through what I went through to understand and bless your people. You have given me more than I deserved and kept me from the penalties of my sins. You loved me even when I didn't love you. You raised me high above my adversaries and protected me from the enemy's schemes. Thank you for keeping me safe. You are a lamp unto my feet and light unto my path. Thank you for saving me from my sins, forgiving me and using me to bless your people. All that's good and perfect comes from you. You're the heart of my contentment, hope for all I do. Jesus you're the center of my joy. I love you and thank you for loving me.

Introduction

Kaleidoscope – Making the Necessary Adjustments to See Yourself As God Sees You was inspired in January 2011, when I was hospitalized and diagnosed with a mild stroke at 49 years old. I knew I needed to make a change, I just didn't like the choices I was given to create that change. But when you don't deal with what's going on, it continues to go on. Our willingness to look at our darkness is what empowers us to change (Iyanla Vanzant).

A kaleidoscope is a cylinder with mirrors containing loose, colored objects. As the viewer looks into one end of the cylinder and rotates the tube in the direction of light, the colored objects overlap and creates various patterns and colors. And so it is with our lives. The events in our lives overlap and form our belief systems and patterns for relating. Those patterns create our experiences, whether beautiful or unpleasant. What you experience produces a feeling and we make decisions based on those feelings, right or wrong.

As you read through these pages, you will see the steps I need to take daily to get to the truth of God concerning me. You've got to be willing to embrace your beauty and look at your ugliness in order to grow. With each Godly revelation, I began to learn about my default responses to circumstances in my life. When we purchase computers, they have default settings automatically assigned to them. In order for our computers to function to our liking, we need to reprogram them. We too have default settings automatically assigned to us (our sin nature) and Jesus is our computer programmer!

As an infant, I had no perception about what disappointments were so my lens, my vision from which I made all choices was without fear. However, as I grew up, disappointments, abandonment, empty promises, abuse and neglect added tiny spots to my lens. This spotted lens is what I use to make decisions for my life. When you do not have a clear perspective about what direction to go in or what decisions to make, you tend to be led by your emotions.

As this revelation started to unfold for my life, I thought about you "my audience." There are so many "Andrea's" out there who fall victim each day to making poor choices for their lives as a result of their pain. We choose not to seek wise counsel because we were taught "you don't talk about what goes on behind closed doors". We fear rejection from others or the pain is best ignored. So we walk throughout life, numb to our sadness, numb to our pain. But you can't break what you don't talk about (TD Jakes). I was concerned about putting my personal business out there to be gossiped about and ridiculed. But the Lord told me that what others say about me is none of my business and that my only concern is to please and obey Him. You, my audience, are worth my level of discomfort in order to save your lives.

The answers to discovering who God needs you to be is revealed in His word, through prayer and wise council. The question is, are you ready to do "the work"? If your answer is yes, remember you can't have your new life and keep your old life. I too was tired of dealing with the same old issues over and over and over again— being sad, depressed, riding that emotional roller coaster, making poor relationship choices, having an unforgiving spirit, not forgiving myself and using other things and people as a crutch to relieve my discomforts. Your circumstances do not have to define you but develop you for who you will be.

I pray you will walk with me through the corridors of my life and take the challenge to examine your default responses to life's mishaps. Purchase a journal so you can reflect in writing your thoughts and emotions. Each day ask the Lord to reveal what each entry could be saying to you. Keep journaling your thoughts throughout the day and pray for revelation. Seek God's word concerning your issues. Don't let fear keep you from receiving all that God has for your life. Take this journey of self-discovery with me. Make a promise to yourself that you are worth the effort. "You must be willing to sacrifice what you value" (Bishop David G. Evans).

"My people are broken - shattered! - and they put on band-aids, Saying, 'It's not so bad. You'll be just fine.' But things are not 'just fine'!" Jeremiah 6:14

CHAPTER ONE

Now Is The Acceptable Time!

hile watching a Reverend Billy Graham taping, he was preaching about being ambassadors for Christ by telling your story, sharing God's word, sharing your life's mishaps, sins, and about God's forgiveness and self-forgiveness. Rev. Graham's sermon was nothing particularly out of the ordinary, for I have heard thousands of sermons similar to his. But one phrase by Rev. Graham changed my perception and gripped my soul—"Now is the acceptable time!"

That phrase was poignant at that particular time in my life because it spoke directly to a struggle I was currently dealing with—my inability to finish and turn over to the editor my already completed book – this book! I've been writing new entries, revising and deleting already written entries because I felt it wasn't appealing enough. I didn't completely understand why I felt unmotivated in handing over this book to my book coach. I've asked many individuals, along with my Bishop David G. Evans and Motivational Speaker Les Brown what they thought was holding me back. They advised me to discipline and set goals for myself each day. They said to do one thing at a time, focus on that and do it well. Have you ever been there before? You know the right thing to do, but after wise counsel you still don't do it?

One day I came across a Marianne Williamson quote, "It is

our light not our darkness that frightens us. Our deepest fear is that we are powerful beyond measure." I asked myself if I was afraid of walking in my destiny and therefore hampered my own progress by avoiding to set goals and discipline myself. Was this the reason I was so stagnant? As I started to journal about yet another area in my life where I needed the Lord's revelation, He started to expose the lies I have been telling myself for four and a half decades – I'm incompetent, unqualified, unworthy of anyone's consistent attention, and no one wants you. These lies made me afraid to move into my destiny so instead I became a perfectionist who rarely accomplishes a goal, people pleaser and self-condemning.

I hear wisdom knocking at the door of my heart and whisper "you are more than a conqueror, God loves you, you are fearfully and wonderfully made by Him, you are the head and not the tail." But I turn away from her because I don't believe her—I don't believe God. It was easier for me to believe my book would be a failure and stay in the dysfunctional thinking I was familiar with than embrace God's truth. What would people say if they didn't like it? What if my books do not sell and I lose money – money I cannot spare? What if it fails and that failure crushes my spirit and paralyzes me from future endeavors?

This way of thinking is destructive to my sense of worth in Jesus Christ. This is why I must choose to take a daily journey with the Lord discovering who I truly am in Him through prayer, Bible study, worship, and spiritual mentoring. I desire to live out the blessings the Lord has for my life but I am not able to successfully do this if I'm rehearsing the enemies lies in my mind. When I decide to lay down worldly affections and low self-esteem on a daily basis, then those old habits of thinking won't be tied to my self-worth and my sense of acceptance won't come from others.

Scripture

"For the Spirit God gave us does not make us timid,
but gives us power, love and self-discipline."

2 Timothy 1:7

CHAPTER TWO

"It Be Callin' Me"

During the 1991 movie "New Jack City," the cocaine-addicted character named Pookie said to Police Office Scotty "it be callin' me man, it be callin' me". He was referring to the voice of crack cocaine in his life and his inability to kick this incessant habit. This scene portrayed occasions in my life when difficult times tempt me to "be callin'" on things or people that give me instant relief but aren't good for my health or psyche. I've learned throughout my Christian life that my proclivities during very challenging times have been to revert back to old mindsets that I've worked so hard to resist and release to the Lord. In the beginning of a struggle, I'm singing the Lord's praises, attending church regularly, praying fervently and quoting scriptures. However, when the struggle seems to be lasting a tidbit longer than my level of comfort, I become discouraged and have a tendency to wallow in self-pity. This place leaves me feeling weak and disarmed against resisting the tugs and wars of my old life. Despite the fact that I pray, read devotionals and the Bible every morning, I still find myself during challenging times inclining my ear to the voice of my past.

After rehab, Pookie decided to help the police by working as an undercover drug informant. Just like so many of us, we put too much confidence in the flesh and expose ourselves too soon to things or people that have so easily entangled us (Hebrews

12:1). Pookie exposed himself too soon and died as a result. We all have the capacity during challenging times to fall prey to self-sufficiency and forget that we can't trust our heart because it is deceitful, who can know it. (Jeremiah 17:9).

Now you might be reading this and think, "I'm not on drugs so therefore this doesn't apply to me." But Isaiah 59:2 says that sin remains in this world, stays in us and separates us from God. You might not be able to relate to Pookie's story but what is that voice that "be callin'" you when you're feeling depressed, hopeless, wronged, alone or frustrated? Could it be the voice of gluttony, compulsive shopping, smoking, drinking, unforgiveness, stealing, dishonesty, suicidal ideation, adultery, fornication, gossip, or jealousy—just to name a few?

The first step we must take is acknowledging that there is a hindrance (our sin nature) in our lives that is causing us to gravitate towards unhealthy choices. Yes, I have a tendency to *fill in the blank* when I'm feeling *fill in the blank*. The second step is to ask the Lord for forgiveness, receive His forgiveness and then forgive yourself. When you choose to not forgive yourself, you become spiritually clogged. How can you fully love others and yourself, when you choose to not allow God, who is love, to love you with His forgiveness? And the last step is take responsibility for your actions. Put into place the steps needed to make healthier choices. These steps could look like: 1) acquiring a wise accountability partner; 2) making time in your life for daily prayer and Bible study time, and being consistent with it no matter how you're feeling; 3) don't subject yourself to stimuli that's going to tempt you – stay away from your temptation!; and 4) attending church regularly. You must spend time with yourself determining for yourself what works best for you. Be willing to take that journey of self-awareness by examining your conscious thoughts and feelings during challenging times.

Scripture

"Cast all your anxiety on him because he cares for you.
Be self-controlled and alert. Your enemy the devil
prowls around like a roaring lion looking for someone
to devour. Resist him, standing firm in the faith,
because you know that your brothers throughout
the world are undergoing the same kind of sufferings.
And the God of all grace, who called you to his eternal
glory in Christ, after you have suffered a little while,
will himself restore you and make you strong,
firm and steadfast."

1 Peter 5:7-10

CHAPTER THREE

The Process of Forgiveness –
Working It Out

Here we go again, another family celebration. I planned to celebrate with my adult-children but their father wants to join us. Why do I have to be in the same space with people who hurt me? He reminds me of my heartache and I am not in the mood to fake smile and have small talk. My adult-children said, "Mom, why don't you want to go? Please, come with us. You'll have fun." Then I heard myself repeating the same words my mom would say to me; "why do I have to explain why I don't want to do, what I don't want to do?"

I struggle with willingly being around individuals who remind me of my pain, my failure, your betrayal and abandonment. When I see him, I question my self-worth, my womanhood. I dislike being around him so why should I subject myself to having him in my space, my head. This is very painful and I don't see a way out.

I pray constantly about the Lord lessening my pain and changing my heart. Then my thoughts shift to ways my ex-husband is going to suffer for what he has done. I knew I needed to be released from this bondage of unforgiveness because it is so unhealthy for me emotionally, physically and spiritually. My thoughts are consumed with his wrongdoing and it makes me depressed and vengeful. When I'm depressed, I feel lethargic.

When I'm lethargic, I'm not motivated to pray or even attend church. When your pain is fresh in your mind and heart, how do you move from that place to a place of peace, forgiveness and love?

James 4:3 states, "When you ask, you do not receive, because you ask with wrong motives…." I knew my prayers were self-centered and not God-centered. I finally got to a place where I thought I was ready to start praying differently and ask the Lord to open my heart to see this situation through His eyes. When you ask the Lord to help you be more like Him, He graciously honors your request. Soon thereafter, the Lord allowed my shortcomings and temptations to rise to the surface of my eyes. I became confused because I didn't understand how asking the Lord to show me the situation through His eyes involved this process. I became very angry because I didn't feel like I should have to change in order for my circumstances to change since I wasn't the one who caused my pain. So I became more angry and rebelled. I reverted back to old behaviors and lifestyles I thought I was delivered from. When I got over being mad at the Lord, I decided to allow Him to begin the process of changing my perspective, once again. He started showing me my unforgiving spirit, how vindictive I was and that others (including my adult-children) were watching how I was going to handle this. I became angry again because I thought "why are you pointing out my stuff, what about my ex-husband?" Then the Lord answered me and said "because others will know you are my disciple because of how you love others" (John 13:34-35), including your ex-husband. Despite the heart-wrenching agony of releasing him from revenge, I took this forgiveness journey with the Lord, one day at a time. Then the Lord had the nerve to say, "You know you are your ex-husband." I said, "What? How is this possible Lord?" He said because he has areas in his life he needs to turn over to me and be forgiven for, and so do you.

One day while watching the news, the Lord illustrated how forgiveness can change the heart of the worst offender. Serial Killer Gary Ridgeway was being condemned verbally by his victims' family in the courtroom. He sat there stone-faced, without emotion or a care. The last person to speak was the father of murdered victim Linda Rule. Mr. Rule told Gary Ridgeway that many people hate you but that he forgave him because that's what God instructs him to do. The stone-faced Gary Ridgeway started to cry. I realized the most heinous of crimes can be forgiven no matter how difficult. While watching that video, I felt Mr. Rule's forgiveness was the bridge for Gary Ridgeway to accept Jesus into his heart.

The Lord is changing my heart one day at a time. When somebody hurts you, they have power over you. When you don't forgive them, they keep the power. There may be remnants of the past that invade my mind at times, but I can smile now because I feel free. And what's most important is, my ex-husband's stepchildren and our children see one another as siblings who get along and enjoy one another's company. Now, that's God!

Forgiveness is a seed. It grows peace, mended relationships, strength, self-control and reciprocation (Matthew 6:14-15). Pull weeds of revenge and plant seeds of mercy. Wait and anticipate a harvest. Your family and you are worth your effort.

Scripture

"Search me, O God, and know my heart; test me and know my anxious thoughts. See if there is any offensive way in me, and lead me in the way everlasting."

Psalm 139:23-24

CHAPTER FOUR

Sitting On Your Blessings

I attended a workshop entitled "No More Drama – Finding Favor in a Hateful Environment". The presenter told a story about how she struggled with sharing her business ideas with her boss because her boss had a habit of taking credit for her ideas.

This example triggered a similar memory from my past experience as a legal secretary. I never worked in the legal profession before so needless to say, I was inexperienced and intimated. I reluctantly asked the assistance of the more experienced secretaries for fear of rejection, sounding stupid or giving them the impression that I wanted their job. The secretaries I approached either didn't have time to help me or they would explain the information in warp speed – too fast for me to write their instructions down accurately. I remember feeling helpless and frustrated until a senior-level secretary overheard my requests and took the time to walk me through step-by-step. And then she offered her assistance for any future requests I had. I remember feeling so appreciative to her and the Lord because He sent her to help me and she obeyed with a cheerful spirit. I don't know if this senior secretary was a Christian or not, but I did find out later that some of the other secretaries who grudgingly helped me or turned me away were Christians.

Let's fast forward 10 years to a time when I was the expert and my co-worker needed me to share some portions of my job responsibilities with her. I never had a problem helping this young lady before until someone told me she wanted my job. Then I started to recollect times when I came to work and could tell someone was in my office. Things were shifted around, books put back in the wrong places, and my notes and rolodex cards were missing. I asked this young lady why she was asking me so many questions. She said the boss asked her to become familiar with some of my responsibilities just in case I was absent. Even though the boss's reasons were logical, I still felt threatened and was very cautious about what I shared. I began answering her questions in warp speed and sometimes I said I was too busy and asked her to come back later. I prayed about the situation and asked a few individuals what they would do if in a similar situation. And the resounding response was to never teach anyone all of your job responsibilities because you will be expendable. Even though I pray, I know now that I didn't wait for the Lord's response. Therefore, I continued to ostracize my co-worker.

During the workshop "No More Drama", the presenter shared her feelings with us about her boss. She too didn't want to share her expertise and held back for some time. But soon she decided to really petition the Lord for an answer to this ongoing problem. The Lord instructed her to not sit on her blessings and to follow His Kingdom principles, which were: focus on God's expectations for you (Romans 8:6); maintain a degree of silence (Proverbs 17:28); see your problems as opportunities (2 Corinthians 5:7); deal with your haters the right way (1 Peter 3:8); follow God's plan for your life (Jeremiah 29:11); live and work right (Matthew 12:33); and be a change agent "(Galatians 5:22). (L. Asare & A. Holder) The presenter went on to say that God knows the plans He has for us. If the problem is in the plan, then the solution is in the plan. As a result of the presenter following these Kingdom principles, she was promoted to a position higher than her boss.

Sitting on my blessings (my knowledge and expertise) out of fear only blocks future blessings. I'm learning each day to walk more boldly by faith and not by sight (2 Corinthians 5:7) because my steps, my path, my job, my future are ordered by the Lord (Psalm 37:23). I must practice being the change I want to see in others. So when I'm challenged in making a decision, I ask myself "where does your strength lie? Is it in your ability to rationalize a problem or your faith in God?

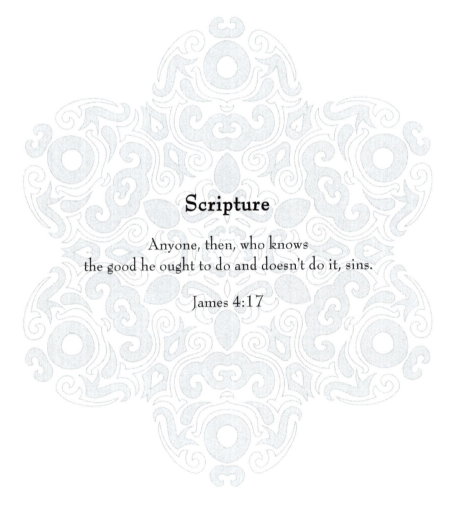

Scripture

Anyone, then, who knows
the good he ought to do and doesn't do it, sins.

James 4:17

CHAPTER FIVE

Slipping into Darkness

Trials are surrounding me like the black plague. I cannot escape and it's making me so depressed. Every little thing that crosses my path seems to slip me deeper and deeper into that abyss. It seems like everything I do to escape is futile. I hate being here. I hate feeling this way. I can't even utter a word of encouragement or prayer for myself let alone for you — that person who's calling me right now on my cell. I can't answer because hearing your complaints will only give me a reason to continue this journey of self-loathing.

Lord, where are you? I know the Word says you will never leave me nor forsake me (Deuteronomy 31:6) but I need to feel you so desperately right now. I feel so alone, scared, unsupported and unloved. I want my mom! Cry cry scream cry. I need a drink! Here I go again, slipping and sliding down that pathway to nowhere but self-destruction. I feel like I'm spiraling out of control and can't seem to get a grip to stop its progression. Lord, save me!

Stop! Look! Listen! The Lord is trying to say something and you can't hear him because you are too consumed with self-thoughts. As I look around, I have an epiphany. Something looks vaguely familiar. I've been here before. I recognize this place. The purpose of this place is to make me distrust my God. This place wants me to feel faithless. What is this place? This place wants me to think I have the ability to solve this God-sized problem instead of waiting and praying. This place is trying to make me feel like I'm a failure. I recognize this place. I've been here before. This place is called F.E.A.R. (false evidence appearing real).

As I slowly acknowledge the destructive purpose of this place called fear, I now recognize another voice beckoning for my attention. As I listen more intently, I feel my purpose for living slowly return. My perception of my circumstances don't seem as bleak as before. I can feel the presence of the Lord embracing my weary soul and my strength, courage and hope reappear. Then I picked up my Bible and read Isaiah 26:3, "You will guard him and keep him in perfect and constant peace whose mind [both its inclination and its character] is stayed on You, because he commits himself to You, leans on You and hopes confidently in You." (Joyce Meyers)

As I come out of the abyss of my own choosing, I start to feel free and liberated because I remembered that I have options. I can either choose to allow the enemy to make me feel hopeless and in despair over the circumstances the Lord has allowed in my life or I can choose to trust in the one who realizes I am equipped for anything He allows. He is the answer to every problem and the solution in every situation. When the Lord allowed hardship to enter my life, it was for a purpose and a plan. Not to destroy me but for an expected end (Jeremiah 29:11).

This is why it is so important to consistently spend time with the Lord especially when we are going through challenging times. You are not that smart, that strong or that savvy to handle life's challenges without the Lord. Remember, "where the mind goes, the man follows." (Joyce Meyers)

Scripture

"Don't be so naive and self-confident.
You're not exempt. You could fall flat
on your face as easily as anyone else.
Forget about self-confidence; it's useless.
Cultivate God-confidence."

1 Corinthians 10:12

CHAPTER SIX

Hiding out in plain sight

Have you ever sat in a crowd of people, laughing, engaged in conversation and all the while hiding your pain, your predicament or your shameful poor choices? While actively interacting with others, you think to yourself "they don't even know who you are." Your mind slips away from the crowd, recollecting certain instances that you're not proud of. Then you discontinue your mind-wandering and join in laughing at whatever was funny because you've mastered the art of hiding out in plain sight. Yeah, never let them see you sweat. Never let them know who you really are. Let them continue to believe you got it going on. Lord knows they could never find out your pain, your predicament or your shameful poor choices because their perception of you would change and you would feel so ashamed. The saddest thing about that statement is "what others would think about you." Shouldn't the most important thing be what the Lord thinks about you and what you think about yourself?

My mind slips away from the crowd once again, thinking, "I wish I could live a life that's tarnish-free—where I didn't have these temptations that pursued me like a rabid dog, that leave me feeling so ashamed." At certain times, that rabid dog seems to catch me more often than I flee it. I pray I will out run it, dipping and dodging down the alleyway of life. Lord, please don't let it catch me this time. Please don't let it outrun and find me out of breath and unable to defend myself from its attack. Then I discontinue my mind-wandering and join in laughing at whatever was funny because I've mastered the art of hiding out in plain sight.

I'm not saying you have to wear your emotions on your sleeves for the world to see. But you can get caught up in being a pretending practitioner with your patented answers and plastered smiles. You wind up fooling everyone around you, sometimes even yourself. Is this any way to live – inside yourself, hiding yourself from yourself? How do I get out of this place?

In order to free yourself from self-loathing, you must first have a desire to change. Change is difficult for the self-loather because he/she is motivated oftentimes by a sense of fear or guilt (*Harvard Women's Health Watch*). Second, seek the advice of a mental health professional to find out where self-loathing comes from. Individuals who self-loath often suffer with low self-worth and feel they don't measure up to society's standards. Anneli Rufus says self-loathing is the greatest bias against yourself (Psychology Today, 2013). Third, you must ask and receive the Lord's forgiveness and then forgive myself. Self-loathing is a trick of the enemy to keep you believing the Lord's forgiveness is insufficient. There must be something else, besides confessing, I need to do in order to be forgiven. Absolutely not! "If we confess our sins, he is faithful and just to forgive us our sins, and to cleanse us from all unrighteousness" (1 John 1:9). Jesus' love sets us free and by receiving it proves I take His seriously.

Scripture

"For those who live according to the flesh set their
minds on the things of the flesh, but those who
live according to the Spirit set their minds
on the things of the Spirit."

Romans 8:5

CHAPTER SEVEN
Guidelines

Ralph Linton stated "The culture of a society is the way of life of its members; the collection of ideas and habits which they learn, share and transmit from generation to generation. Since human beings have no instinct to direct their actions, their behavior must be based on guidelines which are learned."

All of us have a set of guidelines that are passed down to us by those who raised us. As a school counselor, I see hundreds of different norms children adhere to and when I meet their parents, I can see an uncanny resemblance in behaviors, mannerisms and belief systems. I didn't realize until I was much older, how much of my families' norms and styles of behavior were ingrained in me which I have passed on to my children. Some examples of habits and ideas in my family are: saying your grace and prayers, a love for cooking and eating, supportive family system, community service involvement, attending church regularly, dressing a certain way when you attend church, respecting adults, and a love for education.

The above are all good qualities, however, there are some philosophies that have been passed down that are not as constructive. When I think of the different belief systems passed down, it saddens me because my children model some of these same beliefs, such as: fear of expressing one's emotions in public (i.e. crying), tendency to be frivolous with money, having a shame-based disposition, enabling, judgmental, fear of confrontation, bossy, stubborn, turning a blind-eye and a deaf ear to mental illness or drug addiction, to name a few.

Many families will give one another a pass to exercise dysfunctional patterns of behavior because no one wants to challenge themselves and others to change. Each person validates one another's dysfunction. So how can we change these norms that have been passed down and modeled throughout the family for centuries? First, by being brave enough to set a new norm. Doing so will oftentimes leave you out in the cold, defending yourself against those family members who defy change. Some of us are so stuck on having our way that we leave no room for anyone else's perspective, even if your opinion is overruled by the majority. This mindset only perpetuates a dysfunctional norm within the family.

Imagine your family's norms as a large line dance. You have your leaders and you have your followers. Occasionally there's some tricky move throughout the dance that requires some expertise and guidance on the part of the leaders. The followers aren't too concerned because they are used to obeying the voice of the leader. Everyone who participates in this family dance knows their position. Knowing your place is comfortable for the entire family because no one's toes are being stepped on. Everyone gets used to their position until someone gets tired of leading or following. This is when chaos could possibly erupt. Some complaints might sound like: 1) why are we changing, we've always done it this way; 2) this feels too uncomfortable. Let's keep it the same; and 3) you're going to cause a lot of unrest within the family if we change it. And the cycle will continue unless someone is willing to take a stand and break this dysfunctional generational pattern. How has your family's norms and styles of relating benefited or worked against you? What steps do you believe need to be taken in order to break the cycle of dysfunction?

Scripture

"Do not be conformed to this world (this age),
[fashioned after and adapted to its external,
superficial customs], but be transformed (changed) by
the [entire] renewal of your mind [by its new ideals
and its new attitude], so that you may prove [for
yourselves] what is the good and acceptable and
perfect will of God, even the thing which is good and
acceptable and perfect [in His sight for you]."

Romans 12:2

CHAPTER EIGHT

I'm Not Like That, Am I?

Autonomy can be challenging for teens because even though they want the freedom to be independent they still need to depend on their parents. So the tug-of-war begins and can get increasingly challenging on both child and parent as the child approaches adulthood.

My youngest daughter was headed to Savannah, Ga. to complete her Masters in Fine Arts Degree. I was so excited for and proud of her. And then she said her boyfriend was relocating and they would be living together. I immediately thought oh no he's not! I had good reasons why they shouldn't live together not to mention the fact that I believed he would thwart her studies and opportunities. But her mind was made up. I used all types of tactics: promises, scriptures, fasting and prayer, and even asked other family members to talk with her. I was relentless. All to no avail! My child was so stubborn. How can I get her to change her mind?

There is a fine line between thinking you're giving loving advice versus strong-arming another with demands and attitudes. Needless to say, I wore myself out. Nothing was working and that was working my last nerve. While praying one morning about the situation, the Lord spoke to my heart. "You're controlling. You think others should march by the beat of your drum including me." A grimacing look immediately came over my face and I shivered. My mind arrogantly proclaimed, "I'm not like that, am I?" I sucked my teeth and immediately pushed past that comment and thought "that's nothing but the enemy."

I became physically exhausted and my nerves were a wreck. My mind was consumed with thoughts of the "what-if's": what if she misses out on an internship opportunity, what if she gets pregnant, what if they elope." Oh Lord Jesus, please change her mind! Several weeks later, in the wee-hours of the morning, the Lord spoke to my spirit, "I have everything under My control. Leave the subject alone!" I said to the Lord, "are you saying you want me to keep my mouth shut and let You handle it?" The Spirit once again reassured me that no matter what decision my daughter makes, that He had everything under His control.

Exhale! I decided at that moment to truly let it go. At once, I felt the Lord's peace envelop my mind and soul and I knew everything was going to be alright. I felt relieved because I didn't have to carry a burden I wasn't equipped to handle. A week before my daughter left for college, she informed me that her boyfriend decided not to relocate due to unforeseen reasons. I asked her how she felt about it. She said she prayed, asked the Lord for direction and was at peace with the final decision. She was also happy that I finally trusted her to make her own decisions. She said, "mom, I am a responsible adult." I said, "yes you are honey no matter how difficult it is for me to believe you're all grown up. And I'm so proud of you but you'll always be my baby." We embraced and at that moment our relationship shifted.

I must confess that I'm not completed cured of my need to express my opinion in a forthright, pushy manner. With much prayer, I'm learning to respect the decisions my adult children are making for their lives. They too, are working out their salvation with fear and trembling. (Philippians 2:12). Amen!

Scripture

"Trust in the Lord with all your heart
and lean not on your own understanding;
in all your ways acknowledge him,
and He will make your paths straight.
Do not be wise in your own eyes;
fear the LORD and shun evil."

Proverbs 3:5-7

CHAPTER NINE

Planting Seeds for a Season

As a school counselor, my heart aches when I see injustices against our little ones. Neglect, abuse of all kinds, insecurity and fear are what many of our kids see on a daily basis. As I lotion a little boys dry and cracked legs, I realize I can't allow my heart to get too close because this is his reality and it saddens me. Or that little girl who comes to school smelling like urine and her hair is unkempt. She's a target for bullying and now has become the very thing she feared, a bully. No one wants to be near her because her odor permeates the classroom. Teachers don't even want to be near her. My heart has to find a place that my nose can't connect to in order to hug her. Innocent children, ignored by those who are responsible for their wellbeing, shouldn't have to be exposed to so much wrong so early in life.

I want to be his foster mother but the agency is giving me the run-around. His mother doesn't want the responsibility of caring for him which is the reason he is in foster care once again. I want to shelter, feed and clothe him. I want him to feel he is loved. I want to raise him in the nurture and admonition of the Lord. Our little African American boys who struggle educationally, grow up in unstable homes and are exposed to abuse are more likely to lead a life of crime or drug abuse (Centers for Disease Control and Prevention). Finally, the social worker returns my call. I told her if being a foster mother isn't possible, then I would settle for being a big sister to him just as long as I continue to have an influence in his life. She said okay, I will get back to you. But she never did. This cycle of returned telephone calls and empty promises went on for about eight months.

As my heart aches for this little fella, I'm angrily forced to embrace the apparent answer of no. No, I cannot love him. No, I cannot show him a better life. No, I cannot share him with my family. No, I cannot have an influence in his life. I pray and ask the Lord why am I not allowed to love him like a mother should? Then the Lord reveals his answers to me.

The Lord reminded me that I do have an influence in his life, through the many past, present and future prayers and seeds of love and care I have planted. He reminded me to stand firm and have faith in His Word because my work is not in vain (1 Corinthians 15:58). There will be many occasions that I will pray for others and not always see the results. This is why I must consistently study the Word of God especially during times of doubting whether my labor will produce the results I desire.

Then the Lord reminded me of one of my favorite scriptures in Psalm 139:23-24 "Search me, O God, and know my heart; test me and know my anxious thoughts. See if there is any offensive (intrusive, pushy) way in me, and lead me in the way everlasting." Then I had to examine whether the Lord has directed me to be a foster mother. I had reasoned in my mind that this was the best solution for this life particularly since this has been a dream of mine since I can recall. There is nothing wrong with my desire to see this little boy healthy in all areas of his life but I must let the Lord assign his stewards to his life. So now my prayer is, Lord if this is not for me, block it. I cannot run my life successfully apart from the Lord. I must put my confidence and trust in Him. I pray for my little guy often that the Lord will keep him safe and bless his mother with a desire to responsibly parent or that another family will come along and bless him with a loving home. Ms. Brown is always thinking about you. Love you to life!

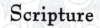

Scripture

"Let us not become weary in doing good,
for at the proper time we will
reap a harvest if we do not give up."

Galatians 6:9

CHAPTER TEN

Do You Remember?

Don't you remember the pain you inflicted on me? Don't you remember the money you owe me? Don't you remember when you rejected me? Don't you remember telling me I would never amount to anything? Don't you remember when you betrayed my confidence? Don't you remember your questionable behavior with my man? Don't you remember smiling in my face right after you slandered my name? I wonder if you remember.

The pain, the disrespect, the heartache, and misery. The embarrassment, the shame, the blame game, the grief. Ripping at my mind, my body, my spirituality, and my soul. Depleting me of every morsel of strength to move past this place of unforgiveness and revenge. I can't move! I can't conceptualize any type of tomorrow that will put a smile back in my heart and on my face. I'm in so much pain and I can't see myself through this place. How could your mistreatment of me work out for my good?

Then the Lord spoke to my spirit: I can identify with your weaknesses (Hebrews 4:15); I can identify with being betrayed (Luke 22:4 & 48); I remember when they made me feel I wasn't worth their effort (Matthew 26:40-43); and I remember when they misjudged me (Matthew 27:22-23). The Lord needed me to know that he sympathized with my pain. There is nothing that's too trivial or too traumatic that the Lord can't identify with. The

Lord said, I know how it is to feel weak (Luke 22:42) and I know what is required to forgive (Ephesians 4:32).

My initial inclination is to feel sorry for myself and wallow in self-pity. And it's a real place to visit when others have treated you unfairly. This is why it is mandatory for me to connect with the Lord and my accountability partners to help me process my many emotions so I can use them as learning experiences and teaching opportunities. (Iyanla Vanzant). Whichever the lesson the Lord has assigned to me, it is essential that I prepare my mind for action; be self-controlled; and set my hope fully on the grace to be given me when Jesus Christ is revealed (1 Peter 1:13 (NIV)).

The next step of this journey is forgiveness. When others harm me emotionally, financially or even spiritually, there is nothing within me that wills to forgive them. Depending on the situation, I might say I've forgiven him/her but there still lies underneath the surface a subtle callousness towards that person. I'm realizing with every offense, forgiveness causes me to enter in to all the purposes God has for me which can be a beautiful experience if I'm willing. Forgiveness is liberating because somewhere within me there is this need to be more than I've allowed myself to be.

Logic will not change an emotion but action will. Forgive!

Scripture

"And when you stand praying, if you hold
anything against anyone, forgive him,
so that your Father in heaven may
forgive you your sins."

Mark 11:25

CHAPTER ELEVEN

It Was Just My Imagination

Are you familiar with the lyrics by the Temptations "It's just my imagination, once again, runnin' away with me" (AZLyrics). This song is about a man's thoughts of a particular woman that passes him every morning. His passion for her takes him to a place where he believes "this couldn't be a dream for too real it all seems." He willingly allows himself to go to a place that affords him the opportunity to live out his fanciful assumptions about this woman.

I remember feeling this strongly about someone once. I would gaze into space, with a smile on my face, and imagine our lives as an admired, loving, married couple. He was strong, intelligent, and God-fearing, and he chose me as his woman. To me, he was the man described in Proverbs 31:23 "Her husband is respected at the city gate, where he takes his seat among the elders of the land." He cares for me, protects and comforts me. I feel safe, adored and loved. He chose me and it felt good! His adoration and love for me was apparent to all!

Your imagination will get you in trouble when you need to find a way around the will of God. If you revisit that mirage over and over again in your mind, sooner or later it will become your reality, even though you know deep in my heart he is not worth your effort. I shutter with disgust because I allowed myself to revisit that lie again. My heart sank and I felt so alone because my reality is nothing like I keep imaging. The pain of that reality exposed those hurtful places in my heart I so strategically try to hide from everyone, including myself. But here I am again, faced with my sad reality that "what I really feel, my eyes won't let me hide because they always start to cry. Cause this time could mean goodbye." (AZLyrics)

Then the Lord spoke to my heart with these words: "your reality is sad because you're making relationship choices through your issues and not my Word." When you decide to ask Me to give you My perspective, then and only then will you see that I'm trying to save you from the tricks of the enemy. This is not the plan I have for you. Please take My hand and trust My Word which is "a lamp unto your feet and a light unto your path." Psalm 119:105

Have you ever made a relationship something that it wasn't? If so, ask the Lord to: 1) reveal to you why you keep choosing the same type of person; 2) give you the strength to receive what He needs you to see about you; and 3) exercise better choices.

Scripture

"For I know the thoughts and plans that I have
for you, says the Lord, thoughts and plans for welfare
and peace and not for evil, to give you hope in your
final outcome. Then you will call upon Me,
and you will come and pray to Me, and I will hear
and heed you. Then you will seek Me, inquire for,
and require Me [as a vital necessity] and find Me
when you search for Me with your heart.

Jeremiah 29:11-13

CHAPTER TWELVE

Is Your Perception Reality?

While attending a woman's event at a church, the moderator decided to take a 15-minute break. During the break, I perused the banquet room, taking in the many conversations the women were engaged in. As I looked around, my eyes fell on two women who appeared to be whispering. The women turned and looked at me and then proceeded to whisper again. I immediately froze my scan and thought "are they talking about me?" I slowly looked over my shoulder to see if they were possibly looking at someone else. There was no one behind me so I discretely worked my eyes back in their direction to see if they were still looking at me. This time, one of the ladies was staring at me over the other woman's shoulder and whispering in her ear. I thought, what in the world is going on. It's a shame some women are always gossiping about somebody.

The moderator asked all women to return to their seats. As I returned to my seat, I felt disturbed and had this unsettling feeling in my spirit. I wondered what was going on and why they seemed to be interested in me. As the speaker continued her presentation, I decided not to be distracted by what just occurred. However, before I knew it, I was daydreaming about what their conversation was about. I tried to focus on the speaker but my mind kept flip flopping between possible scenarios. My thoughts created its own conversation—women are a trip; they don't even know me; I wonder if they are talking about my new boyfriend; wait, they don't even know him. I hated the fact that I was so distracted because it was taking up entirely too much of my time. The more I decided not to be worried about what they were talking about, the more I worried about it. I hated how much time I was wasting on them. Each time I saw those women, I felt an uneasiness in my spirit towards them.

One evening while I was reading scripture, I came across Philippians 4:8. My mind immediately went to the incident of those two, supposedly, gossiping women. And then I asked myself "what is it about me that cares about what two strangers are possibly saying about me?"

When I am faced with situations similar to this, I have to decide not to worry about something until I have something to worry about. What other people think about me has always been a struggle of mine and it has consumed my every waking moment in the past. I must decide to think the best about people and situations, instead of making it drama-filled. The next several times that this happened, I said to myself "what they think about me is none of my business."

Scripture

"Finally, brothers, whatever is true, whatever is
honorable, whatever is just, whatever is pure,
whatever is lovely, whatever is commendable,
if there is any excellence, if there is anything
worthy of praise, think about these things."

Philippians 4:8

CHAPTER THIRTEEN

Don't Fight the Funk

The month of May 2010, was the worst month I could remember ever having in a long while. I couldn't quite put my finger on why but all I knew was I felt like a dismal cloud followed me everywhere I went. Have you ever felt heavy, overloaded, weak, and dismayed? Well, that was me. I couldn't shake this feeling and to be honest, I don't think I even really tried. I tried to smile when all I could do was frown. I tried to laugh when all I could do was cry. And to be honest, it was totally exhausting trying to fight the funk. I knew how to fake it in public, but those who really know me, knew something was wrong.

My prayer partner said, "what is wrong with you? Tell me, you know what it is." But I didn't know or maybe I wasn't ready to face it. Have you ever been there? It's like the answer is down the street and you're squinting trying to make out the image but you refuse to walk towards it to get a better picture. I didn't have enough energy or will to walk towards the answer, and frankly I didn't even care. That's how tired and depressed I was. All I could do was muster enough energy every day to pray and read my Word, go to work, come home, cook dinner, drink my wine and get on Facebook.

And then one day, I woke up. I don't literally mean I woke up from my sleep but I figuratively woke up from depression, irritability, self-loathing and self-destructive. I became a victim of my own choosing. But God, but God, but God! You see, even though I felt the way I had for an entire month, I didn't stop praying, I didn't stop reading the Word, I didn't stop talking to my prayer partner. I was doing something right even though I didn't give it much attention. All I could see was my depression.

Have you ever seen the 1994 movie *Shawshank Redemption*? Remember how Tim Robbins' character "Andy", while in prison, kept chipping away at the wall with his chisel and years later, there it was – his way out of prison and he escaped. That's what prayer, reading God's word and talking to my prayer partner did for me. Without me realizing during my depression, those habits chiseled away at that dismal cloud of depression which hovered over me during that long month of May.

Whenever your emotions are all over the place, you can either choose to ignore what you're feeling, continue to be a grump and make the rest of your day miserable for you and everyone around you. Or you can choose to recognize (if possible) why you are emotional, accept the fact that you're human, decide to be good to you by pampering yourself with the Word of God and prayer, take a lavender bubble bath (or whatever your favorite scent), listen to soft music, enjoy your favorite desert and/or beverage, and try again tomorrow. When I decided to stop fighting the funk, I was able to rest in my humanity. I'm not perfect but the God that I serve is. He understood exactly where I was, what I was feeling, and what I needed, which was time to be. And soon the revelation came – it was Mother's Day, and I missed my mom.

Scripture

"For we have not a high priest which cannot be
touched with the feeling of our infirmities;
but was in all points tempted like as we are,
yet without sin. Let us therefore come boldly
unto the throne of grace, that we may obtain
mercy, and find grace to help in time of need."

Hebrews 4:15-16

CHAPTER FOURTEEN

It Is Not About You

C hristine was one of my Proverbs 27:17 friends. "As iron sharpens iron, so a man sharpens the countenance of a friend." I don't think Chris ever knew she was this type of friend to me. If for any other reasons Chris and I were placed in one another's lives, was that she needed daily support while battling cancer and I needed sharpening.

Chris has been my next door neighbor for about six years. For the last 2-1/2 years, we grew closer than I thought possible because I'm the type of neighbor that usually waves hi and goodbye sprinkled with periodic small talk. There's nothing wrong with that per se; however, when you're a Christian, you are a disciple. And wherever the Lord chooses to use you as His disciple, well, you're supposed to follow His example. John 13:34-35, describes a disciple as one who loves the brethren which is patterned after Jesus. This pattern is visible to all so all will know you are the Lord's disciple.

When Chris needed help, she would send me to the store and asked for specific items, i.e., Poland Springs water, Oatmeal Raisin Cookies or Safeguard soap. If I brought back Oatmeal Cookies, Dasani water or Dove soap, she would say "oh I don't eat Raisin cookies or drink Dasani water. Would you be able to take these back? All I could silently say was "Jesus, keep me near the cross because I just spent almost two hours in Target picking out

30 specific items, mind you, for Chris. And then I thought, "Andrea, you complain a lot. I was more concerned with my convenience than my sister's minor needs. Because you see, her main need was to be healed. I couldn't give her that, so the least I could do was serve her with her heart's desires. I mean, isn't that what we request of the Lord, our heart's desire.

You see, you don't realize how much of an impact a person has in your life until you're about to lose them. I never thought that my relationship with Chris would help me acquire more insight and an ability to express certain feelings about what was going on in my heart.

That's what she did for me. She helped me see another side of me. I pray every morning "Search me [thoroughly] oh God, and know my heart! Try me and know my thoughts! And see if there is any wicked or hurtful way in me, and lead me in the way everlasting." Psalm 139:23-24. I so desire for the Lord to use me and to make me more like Him. I want Him to have me on this level that I have been desiring but, you see, I'm not always willing to do what's required, which is "my reasonable service" (Romans 12:1). That's one thing Chris helped me see. She helped me see my selfishness. "The very essence of ministry requires, first and foremost, a recognition that it's not about you. Effective ministry must necessarily focus, not on the minister and his or her needs, but rather, on those ministered to and their needs." Alfred Darryl Jumper

God calls us to abandon our selfish desires. Only in leaving behind self-seeking ways will we be free to truly serve others.

Scripture

"A new commandment I give unto you,
that ye love one another; as I have loved you,
that ye also love one another. By this shall
all men know that ye are my disciples,
if ye have love one to another."

John 13:34-35

CHAPTER FIFTEEN

Wasted Time?

I was in a relationship for some time with someone who was not the Lord's pick for me. This guy wasn't all bad and had a lot of great qualities. However, I didn't trust him, felt insecure in the relationship, and he didn't pursue the Lord to the point that made me want to follow his leadership. You might be thinking, so you were with him because? I sensed three months into this relationship something about him wasn't quite right, sort of unsettling. But in order for me to stay in this relationship, I had to have an ongoing conversation with myself, which consisted of "he's alright and makes me feel good. He's good with this and he's good with that. He's very likable, engaging and intelligent. He seems willing to change and I believe things will change. What's the big deal after all? It feels good to have a boyfriend, and I deserve to feel good!" Have you ever had an adamant conversation with yourself defending your choices?

Have you ever known in your heart a relationship, a job, or even a pair of shoes wasn't a wise choice, but because your decision crossed a vulnerable time in your life, you went with what made you feel good instead of what made Godly sense? Anyone, anyone?

I anesthetized my Christian instincts and conviction with self-deceit and made the wrong choices. The longer I stayed, the more it seemed like the right decision. But there was a tug of war going on in my Spirit. This should be the case for any Christian who studies the Word of God and prays. I knew this wasn't the man for me, I knew it in my heart. But my desire to be needed was greater than my need to please the Lord.

There are many individuals, including myself, who have kicked themselves for wasting so much time in relationships that were going nowhere. Wasted love, wasted energy and a whole bunch of regrets. But over time, I learned that making poor choices is a part of teaching us valuable life lessons. I no longer consider that relationship a waste of time. Because it took me all those years to learn a few things about myself. I learned why I kept choosing the same type of man, why I stayed in that relationship for so long, and how much I didn't trust the Lord. I thank God I am determined even more to stick to my values, love myself and the Lord. Learning a valuable Godly lesson for a life time – well, that's never a waste of time.

"What is it in us that seeks the truth? Is it our minds or is it our hearts?" (A Time to Kill Quote)

Scripture

"My son, pay attention to what I say; listen closely to
my words. Do not let them out of your sight,
keep them within your heart; for they are life to
those who find them and health to a man's
whole body. Above all else, guard your heart,
for it is the wellspring of life."

Proverbs 4:20-23

CHAPTER SIXTEEN
Misjudged

As a school counselor, I encounter numerous complaints from children that a peer was talking about them and spreading nasty rumors. I usually ask: "did you hear them say this"? The number one response is usually "no, but my best friend told me." And my number one reply is "if you didn't hear the person say this out of their mouth, what makes you think it's true? They usually reply "because my best friend told me and she/he doesn't lie."

Peers play a big part in the social and emotional development of one another. Their influence starts at an early age and increases throughout the teenage years. During this time, the "he says, she says" drama begins. This is expected because their perception of one another is very important during this time but they will eventually grow out of it. Unfortunately, this is not always the case. I have encountered many adults, including myself, that engage in this "he says, she says" drama just like our teenagers. Adults hear a word of gossip and have a desire to spread it like it's the gospel truth. Bertrand Russell said "No one gossips about other people's secret virtues."

I remember a particular time when I was the target of gossip. A friend shared with me the nature of the rumor regarding me. What was most disheartening was, this fabricated lie was being spread by someone I admired. At that point in my life, I was very insecure and needed to believe in something or someone important. And now the image I had of my admired-friend was tarnished. To realize grown folks were gossiping a lie about me made me feel depressed and offended. I held contempt in my heart and judged that person. This incident took me back to a time when I was in sixth grade when a boy spread a rumor that he did something to me sexually. It was a lie but the response from my peers and teachers were so overwhelming that I was unable to defend myself. I just listened to them repeat the lies to my face and never said a word. I told my grandmom I was sick and stayed out of school for two days. Now here I am again, many many years later. I'm reliving these same feelings all over again. I am so angry at myself for not defending myself once again against my adversaries.

Then the Lord reminded me that the enemy's purpose for using people against me is to tear me down, make me feel guilty and unworthy, and it robs me of my faith and confidence in Him. He said remember my words and imprint them in your heart. Do not be afraid of the terror of the night, nor of the arrow (the evil plots and slanders of the wicked) that flies by day (Psalm 91:5) because "He will give his angels charge over me to accompany and defend and preserve me in all my ways (of obedience and service) (Psalm 91:11). When you ingest scripture with confidence and conviction, those words become a joy, strength and delight to your heart (Jeremiah 15:16).

When someone is gossiping about me or I am tempted to gossip about someone, I pray for strength to exercise the Christian response. I strengthen my mind and my heart with the Word of God and the saying, "what others say about me [or what I want to say about someone else] is none of my business!"

Scripture

"Brothers, do not slander one another.
Anyone who speaks against his brother
or judges him speaks against the law
and judges it. When you judge the law,
you are not keeping it, but sitting in judgment
on it. There is only one Lawgiver and Judge,
the one who is able to save and destroy.
But you—who are you to judge your neighbor?

James 4:11-12

CHAPTER SEVENTEEN

Whose Report Will You Believe?

Wow Lord, as I look back on the past two and a half years, when I first started Kaleidoscope, I could not have ever imagined being where I am today. There were so many different paths I thought I should have taken – self publishing or allowing another awesome woman to help me publish. But something kept happening along the way – I would become paralyzed and unable to finish Kaleidoscope. This was very frustrating because I knew in my heart someone needed to be blessed by my testimonies but that wasn't reason enough to finish it.

After my conversation with Linda Eastman and her vision for Kaleidoscope, I looked at the ceiling, clinched my pearls, took a deep breath and let out a loud, long scream. To finally believe that I was worthy of writing a book that would bless others with my testimony was such an overwhelming feeling. I shouted and praised the Lord in my kitchen while I held on to my stove. I had one vision for my book but Linda Eastman took it to another level that I could have never imagined. At that very moment, I connected with the Lord in such a spiritual and powerful way. It felt like He was hugging me with arms measuring 10 feet that wrapped around me several times. I felt so honored, humbled and loved that the Lord wanted to use me in such an awesome way.

Have you ever wanted to accomplish something so badly that it consumed your every waking moment and dreams? It was finally happening for me but once again that insecure voice in my head kept telling me "you're not capable of doing that successfully? You're a nobody! And no one wants to read this book?

When the dust settled, my mind was still searching for the right thoughts. Part of me believed I was unworthy of the Lord's blessings and the other part of me held tight to Jeremiah 29:11. I know the Lord has thoughts of peace, and not of evil concerning me. He wants the best for me and I want to give Him my best. I get sick and tired of those childhood voices creeping into my present day stealing me of opportunities that the Lord has provided for me. Why won't they just go away! It's like my mind is having a child-like, tug-of-war with the enemy of what is already rightfully mine.

Then the Lord said "Just because you don't see it doesn't mean it's not there (Hebrews 11:1). You will either believe in the gifts I have for you and direction I am taking you in or you will believe more in your own sufficiency, fears, and doubts. Then I read Numbers 13 and was immediately convicted because I was like the children of Israel. The Lord promised to bless me but I became too focused on the perceived giants around me. The Lord reminds me, in moments of uncertainty and fear, that He is with me, fear them not (Numbers 14:9). The enemy wasn't the problem, I was.

Scripture

"Pray at all times (on every occasion, in every season)
in the Spirit, with all (manner of) prayer
and entreaty. To that end keep alert and watch with
strong purpose and perseverance, interceding on
behalf of all the saints (God's consecrated people)."

Ephesians 6:18

CHAPTER EIGHTEEN

Why are you mad at her?

My telephone is ringing and it's her again. My heart sank and this feeling of regret came over me. I really don't want to answer the telephone and talk with her because I know what she wants. She's either going to complain about another thing or she's going to ask to borrow money. I pick up the telephone anyway. Hey girl, what's up? She usually starts off her conversation with "nothing much girl." Getting ready to do this, getting ready to do that. And then here it comes – another complaint about someone in her life. Then she usually tops off her complaints with "but you know God's got this."

She is so predictable. She tugs and pulls at my strength. Her spirit is so heavy and usually at the end of our conversation, I'm feeling weary, disgusted and moody. Now her spirit of contempt has jumped on to me. She does this every single time I speak with her. And the ironic thing about that situation is I voluntarily let her vex my spirit every single time.

You see, when I answered the telephone, I gave her permission to disrupt my day. So whose fault is it really? Is it hers or is it mine? She treats me this way because I have taught her how to treat me. She can't disrupt my day unless I let her. She can't weigh me down unless I let her. I could have chosen to allow her call to go to voicemail. What is it about me that once I have been convinced of a person's negative habits, I choose to ignore it and continue to allow them to steal my joy. Isn't that called insanity – doing the same thing over and over again and expecting different results?

So I asked myself why I kept doing this. One reason was my need to please people and to be needed. Frank Weed (1983) calls individuals like me "feeling-swallowers." Feeling-swallowers ... swallow their feelings. They smile even if the situation is causing them pain and distress. They behave this way because they consider the approval of others more important. They feel it would be dangerous to affront others by revealing their true feelings.

I am so tired of giving in to other's requests of me. The thing about it is she doesn't know I'm home so the pressure isn't the same as if someone knocked on my door and saw my car outside or heard my television on. The truth of the matter is the issue isn't her, it's me and my inability to be honest with myself about whether I don't feel like being burdened. It is my fault that I allow others to put unrealistic expectation on my time and life.

I realize my habit of swallowing my feelings is something I still struggle with. However, despite my fear of rejection and need to enable, I choose daily to exercise choices that are Christ-like, freeing, uplifting, responsible, and which promotes my wellbeing. I choose to not let fear be my guide.

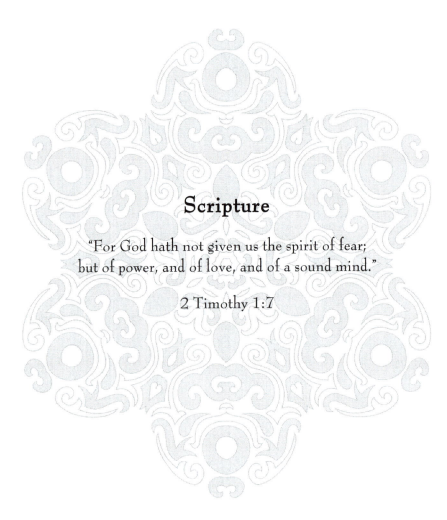

Scripture

"For God hath not given us the spirit of fear;
but of power, and of love, and of a sound mind."

2 Timothy 1:7

CHAPTER NINETEEN

Pain in my Neck

I can't seem to get rid of this pain in my neck and back. Doctors are trying all sorts of medications to relieve my symptoms. Am I doing something wrong, again? The reason I say again is I've learned, from the past, stress has had a lot to do with many of my physical challenges.

I remember this particular time being admitted to the hospital for a possible stroke which turned out to be complex migraines. My best friend, Tina, was visiting me when my father rushed into my room like he was on a mission. He stood in front of my bed, arms folded and lips perched. I immediately knew he had something on his mind and he was going to share it with his daughter. I needed to brace myself because whenever dad was displeased with my circumstances, he perched his lips and started sentences off with "ah ha, you know what,..."

Dad was concerned about my physical state and he knew I was running myself in the ground. As I allowed him to share his heart, I glanced over at my girlfriend to see if she would rescue me. Well, she was nodding in agreement, with perched lips too, so I knew she wouldn't help. In my heart, I knew dad was right but my stubbornness kept me from fully conceding or contemplating an alternative lifestyle.

Have you ever known in your heart you were doing something that didn't benefit your health but you kept doing it anyway? I asked myself, "what is it about you that won't permit yourself to slow down? Why do you choose to stay ignorant to the effects of your actions? Do you not love yourself enough to sacrifice for you? You sacrifice for everyone else, why aren't you on that list?"

Are you people-pleasing again and can't seem to say no? Is your busyness linked to your identity or self-worth? Is it because you don't want to think about your loneliness? Going to a counselor helped me realize if I stayed busy enough, I wouldn't have to face the many issues troubling my heart. I don't know all of the reasons why I do what I do but what I have decided to do differently is ask the Lord for wisdom (James 1:5), knowledge and understanding regarding my lack of knowing why I do what I do. Sometimes asking the Lord doesn't give me microwavable answers but I'm choosing to petition Him for revelation daily. I'm so tired of being ignorant to the effects of my choices.

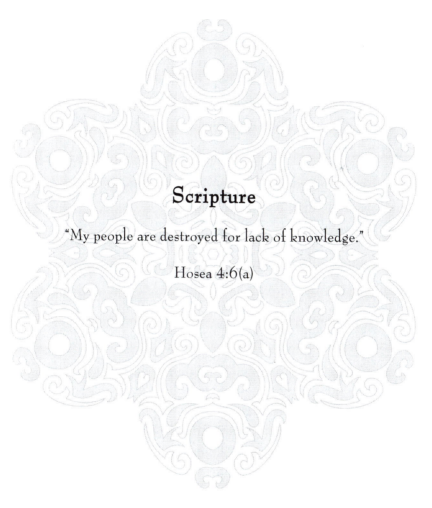

Scripture

"My people are destroyed for lack of knowledge."

Hosea 4:6(a)

CHAPTER TWENTY
Inconvenient Opportunity

While sitting at the lunchroom table, I decided to put my earplugs in and listen to some music so I could block out the background noise in order to get some writing done. I was in my groove and felt good about the writer's flow I was on. I especially felt good because too often I have experienced writer's block and am very disappointed when this occurs. So I was especially excited because I was in my groove.

I could faintly hear others talking in the background but not enough to bother me. Then I felt a tap on my arm. I remembered feeling particularly annoyed because I thought "who's bothering me? Don't you see the earplugs in my ears?" She said "hey girl, I was talking to you." I thought "are you serious? I have earplugs in my ears and you're talking to me?" I said "oh I didn't hear you, I'm listening to my music while I'm writing." You won't believe what happened next. She kept right on talking. I think I was looking at her cross-eyed because I was baffled that she chose to be so inconsiderate. Every time she turned to talk to someone else, I immediately hurried and put my earplugs back in my ears so I wouldn't lose my writer's flow. Two minutes later, here she comes again, tapping me on my shoulder. Jesus keep me near the cross, I screamed to myself!

When I set out to focus on a project and I get into a groove, it seems like people gravitate towards me. I don't know what it is about me being preoccupied that motivates people to talk to me. I become so irritated and annoyed and it takes everything in me to not let these emotions control my disposition. It just so happens that this young lady was going through a trying time. At the end of our conversation, she said, "I knew I could talk to you."

Later on that day, the Lord reminded me of my prayer last week, "Lord please help me not miss an opportunity to serve your people." I thought in an irritated way "did I pray that?" I laughed because I knew I had prayed it but didn't feel like being there for anyone at that particular time. The Lord reminded me that he would position me when I'm needed and it's not about my convenience but about an opportunity to serve His people. I felt convicted because some people will never read the Bible or attend church and the only word they will hear, or image of Christ they will see will come from His saints. The Lord shared with me that so many are hurting and have no hope. It was no coincidence that I sat next to that young lady. It was not by coincidence that she was persistent in wanting to talk with you. The Lord said, "if you really want to follow My example, you have to look outside of yourself and your present circumstances, and serve Me by serving others.

The following week I was at the hairdresser. While under the dryer, I started writing and was in my writer's groove again. An elderly lady sat next to me and asked what I was writing. I answered with a rather lengthy response and then continued writing. She tapped me on my hand and said, "could I run something by you that's been bothering me?" (I smiled and my spirit uttered "Yes, Lord.") That conversation lasted the whole time I was under the dryer. Thank you Lord for another opportunity to serve Your people. Lord, I give my writing to you!

Bishop David G. Evans said during a sermon "divine opportunity is always inconvenient." (January 27, 2013)

Scripture

"[Not in your own strength] for it is God
Who is all the while effectually at work in you
[energizing and creating in you the power and desire],
both to will and to work for His good pleasure
and satisfaction and delight."

Philippians 2:13

CHAPTER TWENTY-ONE

Entitlement Mentality

I've been in the hospital more times than I'd like to admit. I remember being in the hospital once for three days and I only had two visitors. I remember thinking when others are in the hospital, I'm "Johnny-on-the-spot." I'm right there, doing errands, buying breakfast or lending a listening ear. But when it comes to me, I can't seem to get more than two familiar faces to come and see about me. I started to sulk, get annoyed and depressed because I felt unloved. I received a few telephone calls from folks promising to see about me the next day. No visitors the next day.

The Lord said, "yes, they didn't visit you, yes, they didn't connect with you until after you were released. Yes, they don't treat you like you treat them. But I am here and those I sent to visit you." My heart utters, but what about Matthew 7:12, "So then, whatever you desire that others would do to and for you, even so do also to and for them, for this is (sums up) the Law and the Prophets." Then the Lord said "My Word never guaranteed they would be there for you, it just commands you to treat them like you want to be treated."

The Lord said, "your circumstance looks vaguely familiar to Me. It's how you treat me. You don't visit Me when I need you to connect with Me. You connect with Me after you've connected with everyone else. I'm the last person on your list. And yes, you don't treat me like I treat you. You are ungrateful just like many are to you. But I still love you and give to you without reservation. Can you pass that same mercy onto those who didn't visit you?" After being discharged, I became bitter and angry again. I decided I wasn't going to care about others like I did before. I knew my heart wasn't right but I didn't care.

While driving down the street the next week, thinking about nothing in particular, the Lord spoke to me and said, "everyone has their gifts and talents. Do these people you hold contempt for do other things for you that you haven't done for them? You're so focused on someone not visiting you and holding it against them that you will miss out on future blessings from them and Me. Someone might not have a gift of visiting but maybe their gift is fervently praying for you, cooking a meal for you, slipping you some money to pay a bill, sending flowers to you, or going grocery shopping for you."

Having an entitlement mentality is the same as having a prideful attitude. Having this mindset is an indication of where you are spiritually and how much Word you haven't been applying to your life. "Attitudes begin in the mind. Reading the word daily renews our minds and changes our attitude." (The Everyday Life Bible)

Scripture

"Strip yourselves of your former nature which
characterized your previous manner of life
and becomes corrupt through lusts and desires
that spring from delusion; and be constantly
renewed in the spirit of your mind, and put on
the new nature created in God's image in
true righteousness and holiness."

Ephesians 4:22-24

CHAPTER TWENTY-TWO

Liar, Liar, Pants on Fire!

I was sharing a dilemma with a friend about my boyfriend's suspicious behavior and how much I didn't trust him. During the conversation, my friend asked me "Why would you want to be in a relationship with someone you don't trust and who is a liar?" That question felt like a Mike Tyson vs. Trevor Berbick Heavyweight knockout. Her words caught me off balance. I felt dizzy and out of sorts. I couldn't hear anymore and ended the conversation.

I'm sure Trevor Berbick thought "why didn't I see that punch coming? I've been trained to notice those sneaky left hooks before. What happened?" Berbick defeated Ali, so he was the champ. But what was it about Tyson that caught him off guard? Was it fear, weakness, or intimidation? Did he become too confident in his ability to defeat his opponent? Second round, six minutes and five seconds, Tyson catches Berbick off his A-game and Berbick couldn't recovery from the blow. And the thing about that short, left hook, it didn't take much because Berbick was already weak and unprepared.

As Christians, it is mandatory for us to be on guard against anything or anyone that compromises our Christian integrity and common sense. When a challenge displays a weakness within us that is a warning sign that we need strengthening in that area. Blatantly ignoring a weakness is a sign of immaturity.

It is imperative and sometimes a matter of life or death, that we recognize God's warning signs about a situation, a person's conduct or patterns of behavior. The Lord was sending me warnings signs about this guy and I didn't want to see it. I choose to quench the Holy Spirit's voice because my desire was to stay in that dysfunctional relationship.

How do we mature as Christians? By allowing the Word of God to work in our lives each day. We do not have to allow our old mindsets to affect our Christian walk. This is why it is important to have our minds renewed daily so Christ can think and speak through us.

Scripture

"I beseech you therefore, brethren, by the mercies of God, that ye present your bodies a living sacrifice, holy, acceptable unto God, which is your reasonable service. And be not conformed to this world: but be ye transformed by the renewing of your mind, that ye may prove what is that good, and acceptable, and perfect, will of God."

Romans 12:1-2

CHAPTER TWENTY-THREE

Impulsive Shopping

Have you ever gone to the grocery store hungry? I have, numerous times and regretfully ended up with items in my shopping cart that I normally wouldn't purchase. After tasting the items I purchased impulsively, I was disappointed because it wasn't as good as I thought. The only reason why I settled for those items was because I allowed my hunger pains to dictate my choices. When I go to the market with a satisfied appetite, my selections are wise because they are based on careful selection.

This example reminds me of choosing a relationship when you're hungry for affection, companionship and affirmation. You realize your selection was hasty but you settled because it's exciting and feels good. What do you think you are compromising by settling for someone based on emotion only? You are compromising self-love. When you don't love yourself fully, you invite others into your life to treat you with that same level of love, if not worse. If you compromise your standards it will show in their treatment towards you. When others treat you with disrespect, there is something about you that is giving them permission to do so. If you continue to allow others to treat you with disrespect, each time they are around you, they will take a little bit of your soul each time. (Maya Angelou)

When you begin to realize he's not worth your time, don't be bitter at him for mistreating you. He's only doing what he's always done. If this is who he is, believe him! If you know a person isn't treating you fairly and you continue to allow it, whose fault is it? Be mad enough at yourself to demand a change. You are in control of your choices and no one else.

The next time you are contemplating a relationship, pray and study God's word about what type of man God wants for you. Then write out a list of non-negotiables for that relationship. This is a list of what you honestly need in a relationship to stay in that relationship. If you desire a Christian mate, why date an atheist? If you desire an employed mate why date someone with a history of being unemployed and living with their mother. If you desire someone who loves children, why date someone who doesn't have a relationship with theirs? These are all subtle hints to a person's character, life choices and consistent behavior. I'm not saying all individuals unemployed and living with their mother or not having a relationship with their children is not beyond their control because times are hard and things do happen. I'm just saying, watch the consistency or inconsistency of a behavior in your potential mate.

We all need something from one another to stay in relationship with them. Make sure you aren't selling your soul based on short-lived hunger pains. (Genesis 25:29-34) You might not know everything you want in a relationship but based on experience, you should know what you don't want.

If you don't stand for something, you'll fall for anything. (Malcolm X)

Scripture

"Let no man deceive you with vain words:
for because of these things cometh the wrath
of God upon the children of disobedience.
Be not ye therefore partakers with them."

Ephesians 5:6-7

CHAPTER TWENTY-FOUR

Will I go 'round in circles?

Here I am again, laid-off. Here I am again, struggling financially. I don't know where I am emotionally. I feel like I'm in a small boat, in the middle of the sea with no shoreline in sight. I paddle to the north, south, east and west but with no results. I'm tired. Wait, I think I'm supposed to paddle in this direction, it feels right, I think. I'm tired again. Lord, I'm trying to rest in You but I feel like I need to be busy doing something. What that something is, I don't know. Why is it so difficult for me to just let You direct my path? I feel like if I'm not busy doing something, then I'm useless. When and where did I decide that being inactive was useless? Or when did I decide that being busy was useful? When did I get tripped up into believing my way was better? It feels better being proactive but being proactive has left me feeling confused. I need to get busy about the Lord's business and not sit idle doing my business and getting no results.

The word of God says, "In all my ways acknowledge Him, and He will direct my path. Be not wise in my own eyes." Prov. 3:6-7. And further down it says in verses 13 and 14, "Happy is the man that finds wisdom and the man that gets understanding, for the merchandise of it is better than the merchandise of silver and the gain thereof than fine gold. She is more precious than rubies and all the things thou canst desire are not to be compared unto her."

I know if I wait on the Lord, he will renew my strength. I know this. The waiting feels unbearable at times. It's like I can't stand being still. What is that all about? There's a place that the Lord wants me to reside in. It's a place that has peace as its windows and the doors of understanding. It's a place where there is no concern because I know the Lord's got it all under control. It's a place that brings a smile to my face, not from what I can see, but from what is to come. I can speak to my circumstances with confidence because the Lord's word is true. (Isaiah 55:10-11) It says speak those things that be not, as though they were. (Romans 4:17) It's like time-traveling into your future and witnessing the miracle of your situation and then going back in time and rejoicing about it.

So meanwhile, I will take this journey one day at a time, moment at a time and continue to read God's word which is strength for my soul and encouragement for my heart. This is something that I know but fail to exercise. Lord please help me exercise and strengthen my mind, heart and soul with your Word.

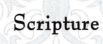

Scripture

"Wait on the LORD: be of good courage,
and he shall strengthen thine heart:
wait , I say, on the LORD."

Psalm 27:14

CHAPTER TWENTY-FIVE

Dearly Departed

One day while sitting in my bedroom, I looked around at all the stuff the Christian speaker Joyce Meyers told me to get rid of. You know that stuff you haven't used in years, or those clothes you're never going to wear again, or those magazines that keep piling up because of that one featured article you're never going to read. I didn't realize how much stuff I had accumulated until my girlfriend Tina asked me one day if I had hoarder tendencies. What?!!? I immediately became defensive because I never ever considered myself to be like those individuals on the television show "Hoarders." After Tina left, I was still angry with her until I allowed that realization to sink in – I have hoarder tendencies.

According to Dr. David Tolin, director of the Anxiety Disorders Center, there are many reasons individuals hoard. **Perfectionism**: If a person cannot make the right decision, they avoid making it at all. **Avoidance**: Individuals avoid taking the chance of throwing something away that could be useful in the future. **Attachment**: Individuals hoard because there is an emotional attachment to the object which could remind them of someone or a happy time. This is usually common among children who moved a lot growing up and their precious childhood items were misplaced or lost. This attachment could be dated back to an earlier period particularly associated with the death of a loved one or there's a history of loss. Loss is a pretty common connection with hoarders. According to the Hartford Hospital, there were over two million people in the U.S. suffering with this disorder. (Oprah, Why Do People Hoard.)

After much prayer, I decided to ask a friend to hold me accountable for my hoarder tendencies. I decided to challenge myself with a small task. I needed to organize my plastic container cabinet because I had over 30 lids that did not have a matching container. My accountability partner advised that I throw away all lids that did not match a bottom. After matching all lids with their respective bottoms, I struggled with throwing away the mixed-matched lids because I thought I might need it one day. My accountability partner sternly advised that I throw them away. I knew he was right but throwing the lids away brought me too much anxiety. I avoided this for two months until I decided to pray about giving my anxiety to the Lord. I started studying scripture pertaining to anxiety. Psalm 94:19 helped me begin the process of releasing this habit to the Lord. "When anxiety was great within me, your consolation brought joy to my soul." I needed my anxiety released by the joy of the Lord. I decided to step out on faith and throw the lids away. An unspeakable comfort calmed my nerves. Even though I know the Lord answers prayers, I was astonished at how quickly His peace enveloped my mind and soul.

Following through with my next task didn't take as long as the first one. I had magazines dating back to 2009 neatly piled high next to my recliner. I haven't thrown them out because there were important articles I needed to read. Thinking about throwing away my magazines brought me a lot of anxiety. I told my accountability partner to hold me accountable for throwing away my magazines. He said he would give me three days to discard them or he would. The next day, I went through the pile of magazines and found myself saying with each magazine "I needed to read that article, I can't throw this magazine away because I might not be able to find this information anywhere else," or "this magazine is a keepsake because Michael Jackson, Whitney Houston or Princess Diana are on the cover." I knew if I hadn't read these articles by now, I wouldn't read it. I petitioned the Lord for His strength and decided any magazine dated before 2013, had to be thrown out. It's a step, right?

As a mental health counselor, I understand the steps I must take to manage this disorder – choosing to expose myself to short-term bouts of anxiety by not exercising my obsessive and compulsive habits. Refusing to face bad habits by keeping my head in the sand doesn't do anything but create a new problem: sand in my hair. John 14:16-17 calls the Holy Spirit "the Spirit of Truth." The Holy Spirit resides in the believer continuously, and desires to bring us to new levels of awareness by shedding old mindsets and habits.

As I conquer each area in my home that needs order, I decide each time not to allow the enemy to control my life by having a faulty, anxious-filled mindset. I instead pray and ask the Lord to help me overcome what I cannot control.

Scripture

"Do not be anxious about anything,
but in everything, by prayer and petition,
with thanksgiving, present your requests to God.
And the peace of God, which transcends all
understanding, will guard your hearts
and your minds in Christ Jesus."

Philippians 4:6-7

CHAPTER TWENTY-SIX

Sovereign

One evening as I scanned my bedroom, my eyes rested on a white and green envelope, about 4-1/2 inches thick that has been behind my bed for almost nine years. Why haven't I been able to get rid of it? When I look at that envelope, I feel so sad, so angry and then depression starts to fill my space. Even though that envelope represented a time in my life that was most painful, I still choose to hold on to it. Have you ever held on to something or someone that has a history of bringing you pain that you find difficult getting rid of?

I will never forget the year 2003. Everything that had the potential of being out of control, was out of control. My marriage was in trouble but I choose not to focus too closely on why because I was dealing with the pregnancy of my daughter, who was a freshman in college, my son's rebellion, and my mom's lymphoma diagnoses. I honestly couldn't muster enough energy to focus on the troubles in my marriage, yet again! Lord, if you allow one more thing on my plate, I feel like I'm going to lose it.

After mom died (the 'one more thing' the Lord allowed), I felt so empty and confused. Why am I the only one in my family who lost her mother at a young age and now the only other woman who ever loved me unconditionally, my mom. Why does my life represent so much loss? How can I move forward when I feel like the weight of another major death is too heavy to bear? The funeral is over and everyone is gone, getting back to life, getting back to reality. But what is my reality now that a major influence and love of my life is no longer here? So many questions, so little answers.

The contents of the green and white envelop contain the medical records of my grandmom, Virginia Mance, whom I called mom since my mother died in 1969. I hate the fact that grief grips my soul to the point it negatively controls my mood, disposition, and even my faith. As I look at the green and white envelope, my mind says: "Here-in lies the medical records of Virginia Mance's last 30 days on earth." I feel like I cannot discard them because maybe one day I will be able to use the records to vindicate her negligent death by that hospital, even though the lawyers said it wasn't a slam dunk case and turned me away.

In the middle of all those realistic but defeating thoughts, the Lord allows Psalm 115:3 to humble me, "Our God is in heaven; he does whatever pleases him." And then the Lord comforted me with Lamentations 3:22-23 "It is because of the Lord's mercy and loving-kindness that we are not consumed, because His [tender] compassions fail not. They are new every morning; great and abundant is Your stability and faithfulness." So today, my soul is renewed and strengthened because of His unfailing love.

Nicole B. Simpson's book Dare 2 Dream states "You can dare to dream by facing all of your traumatic experiences, acknowledging their impact and moving forward in spite of whatever injuries or pain you've suffered" (p. 25). Embracing the Lord's will for my life has not been an easy process because my will is in constant competition against His will (Galatians 5:17). But I choose daily to acknowledge my pain, my wrongdoing, my grief, my idiosyncrasies, and independence from the Lord. And prayerfully during this process of getting to know me, I get to know God. And the Lord reassures my spirit that He will take my heartache and turn it into miracles, if I continue to trust confidently in Him. He says, "Now go and share your testimony, of how I strengthened you, with My people.

Scripture

"We are assured and know that
[God being a partner in their labor]
all things work together and are [fitting into a plan]
for good to and for those who love God and are
called according to [His] design and purpose."

Romans 8:28

CHAPTER TWENTY-SEVEN

Cycle of Shame

Many years ago I was guilty of a particular sin. I didn't make that unwise choice once but many times before. The only difference this time was my sin was found out. As a result of some Christians finding out, they started treating me with indifference. The thing that was so hurtful was the individuals I considered to be my mentors and I admired were the ones treating me with indifference. I decided to follow suit and looked upon them with indifference because of how they treated me. Each time I saw them, I was reminded of my sin and the cycle of shame continued.

I walked around feeling condemned and couldn't forgive myself for many years. I hated the fact that I carried such a heaven burden. I pleaded to the Lord to forgive me for years. One day while attending Philadelphia Biblical University's class on forgiveness, I started to learn and accept the fact that Christ already forgave me and there was nothing further I needed to do.

During this process, the Lord revealed to me that I had been very judgmental and gossiped about other people's sins, and they too felt ashamed and unworthy of forgiveness. When evil words pass our lips, they are indicative of what we harbor in our heart. I now regret making others feel like I felt. I asked the Lord to forgive me and prayed for those I hurt. I don't think I would have realized how judgmental I was until I experienced the same treatment.

The enemy's tactic is to get me to believe that the sin debt the Lord paid for still has a balance due. The devil's strategy is to keep me bound and stagnant from growing and serving the Lord. The only way I can combat the enemy is to stop giving him my mind to manipulate and control. When this occurs, my feelings of inadequacy, shame and guilt dictate my belief system. I must not live by my feelings but live by the Word of God. If I do this frequently, my feelings will start to align with what God's Word says about me. There is nothing that I have done wrong that Jesus has not already fixed through the shedding of His blood.

Scripture

"...But where sin increased,
grace increased all the more."

Romans 5:20(b)

CHAPTER TWENTY-EIGHT
Unqualified

In my history of dating, I have occasionally chosen men who only presented well on the outside. Their presentation at times was the only thing I needed to begin a relationship. And even though my soul searched for a deeper knowledge of who they were, I couldn't allow myself to go deeper for fear of having to decide to be alone. These men committed with their words but were not ready to commit in action. What I mean by action is there were things I would ask of them that would make me feel comfortable so I would stay in the relationship. They would either decide to appease my rant with minimal action or no action at all. I guess they figured out early on that I wasn't going to end the relationship so giving less than stellar effort by them was sufficient.

Early on in the relationship, my spirit and intuition were giving me little glimpses of who they really were. I knew deep in my heart something wasn't quite right. After ending the relationship, I reread some of my old journal entries and discovered that I had inclinations they weren't right for me early on in the relationship. When people show you who they are, believe them. (Maya Angelou) I unfortunately choose not to believe them and wound up learning valuable lessons about why I held on to men who weren't qualified for my life.

I began to ask myself why I was choosing the wrong men. Was I uncomfortable with being alone to the point that I tolerated unacceptable behavior and disrespect? Why didn't I love myself enough to challenge myself to stick to my standards and not settle for less? Because I didn't have clear standards. That's why you must have clear standards for what you need in a relationship and stick by them. Because if you do, you will recognize when others are trying to impose constraints on your life. Settling for less than God's best is disrespectful to you and the Kingdom principals the Lord has set for your life.

Thank God I was finally willing to pray and allow Him to open my eyes in areas where I was deceived (Psalm 109:22). I began to do the hard work to find out why I prematurely qualified men who interviewed well, looked the part, and had great references but had unsatisfactory job performance. I realized I was motivated by the little girl who felt abandoned due to her mother's death and was searching for her father's love and attention. She was searching for someone to love her and make her feel she was worth someone's effort. That type of assurance and security can only come from the Lord because He is the only one who can love us unconditionally. Our Lord knows the truth of each situation, the hearts of people around us, and our own attitudes and motives.

I started to walk more securely as God's leading lady when I decided not to choose men based on my fears, loneliness, rejection, or low self-worth. I am worth the wait. Maureen Dowd said it best, "the minute you settle for less than you deserve, you get even less than what you settled for."

Scripture

"However, as it is written: "No eye has seen,
no ear has heard, no mind has conceived
what God has prepared for those who love him,
" but God has revealed it to us by his Spirit.
The Spirit searches all things, even the deep things
of God. For who among men knows the thoughts
of a man except the man's spirit within him? In the
same way no one knows the thoughts of
God except the Spirit of God."

1 Corinthians 2:9-11

CHAPTER TWENTY-NINE

What will your last words be?

One day while visiting my neighbor-friend Christine, who was dying of cancer, I decided to pray for her. While I was praying, I could vaguely hear her soft, weak, trembling voice say "forgive me Lord, save me Lord, this is hard Lord but thank you Lord." Her words gripped my soul. She was preparing herself to meet her God by making sure there was nothing between her and her Savior. I've often wondered at times about those whose death seems to be prolonged, whether or not the Lord is holding some back until they settle unresolved things in their spirit. I don't know if this was the case for Christine because she was a regular church attendee and served on many committees. We also had long talks at times about the goodness of the Lord. I'm no Bible scholar or equipped to begin to think I know what the Lord is up to in the lives of others but this is what I felt at that moment, at that second. It was like the Lord was embracing Christine, and with her words "forgive me Lord, save me Lord, this is hard Lord but thank you Lord, she was embracing Him back.

While Christine was crying through her pain, I could tell those few words had worn her out. Chris' sister/caretaker, Linda, pressed the medication pump and Chris started to relax. Everyone walked out the room but I couldn't move. I just kept saying Jesus, Jesus, Jesus while the tears rolled down my eyes. You see, it is very difficult seeing someone you've grown to love over the years dwindle physically. That's my neighbor-friend who I shopped for, I stocked her cabinets with food, I washed her dishes and cooked for her. (She loved my fried pork chops and collard greens.) That's my neighbor-girlfriend.

After my visit with Christine, I wondered what my last words would be. Will they be filled with questions of whys and what ifs coupled with an angry disposition? Or will I be like Christine and make sure no offensive stone is left unturned and choose to praise the Lord, even in inevitable death?

Thank you Lord for allowing me to witness Christine's relationship with You. She truly exemplified a woman of Godly character who focused her mind and spirit on You. Her mission during trying times was to know Your character, ways and will, so she would experience Your peace.

I love you Christine, rest in peace my neighbor, my friend.

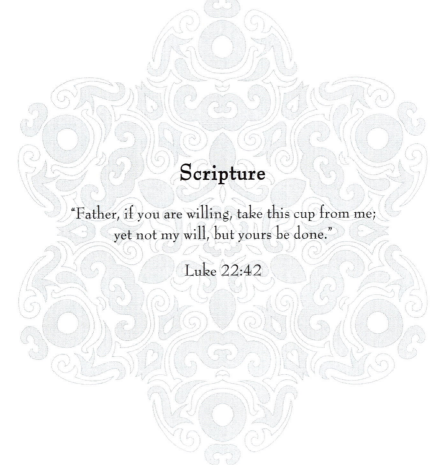

Scripture

"Father, if you are willing, take this cup from me;
yet not my will, but yours be done."

Luke 22:42

CHAPTER THIRTY

Christine 101

Many students who attend college are eligible for Credit for Prior Learning. This program affords students opportunities to receive college credit by taking an exam in the area of their proficiency. When I think about prior learning as a Christian, I wonder what exam the "University of Jesus" would say I'm eligible for?

I didn't realize until I met Christine that I needed to take the Christine 101 course. The objective of this course was designed to assist me in achieving a disciple's attitude and heart. I pray every morning "Search me [thoroughly] oh God, and know my heart! Try me and know my thoughts! And see if there is any wicked or hurtful way in me, and lead me in the way everlasting." Psalm 139:23-24. I wanted the Lord to use me and to make me more like Him but I didn't realize before taking Christine 101 that I was not prepared to fulfill this responsibility nor could I be trusted not to quit mid-stream.

Christine 101 taught me how to exercise Biblical principles on a daily basis in order to demonstrate patience, selflessness and a humble spirit with others. In order to accomplish this, I must cloth myself daily with a "heart of compassion, kindness, gentleness, patience." Colossians 3:12-14. This can only be done through spending quality time with the Lord through prayer and Bible study.

Remember to exercise the very attributes you expect from others.

"How far you go in life, depends on you being tender with the young, compassionate with the aged, sympathetic with the striving and tolerate of the weak and strong, because someday in your life you would have been all of these." George Washington Carver

Scripture

"I therefore, the prisoner for the Lord,
appeal to and beg you to walk (lead a life) worthy
of the [divine] calling to which you have been called
[with behavior that is a credit to the summons to
God's service. Living as becomes you with
complete lowliness of mind (humility) and meekness
(unselfishness, gentleness, mildness), with patience,
bearing with one another and making allowances
because you love one another."

Ephesians 4:1-2

CHAPTER THIRTY-ONE

Offense

Offense means something that causes a person to be hurt, angry, or upset. Everyone at some point in time have been offended by the actions of another. I can think of hundreds of occasions that I've been offended. But there is one particular offense that I would consider the most grievous of all. The worse offense ever occurring in my life was by a young lady whose actions were cold, calculating and heartless towards me. She meant me harm and told me to my face in an elusive and calm manner. She didn't care that she was offensive and made excuses for what she was doing. I was caught off guard by her cunning speech and am sorry now that I spoke with her face to face. But I wanted to come to an understanding about what was going on because I needed answers. Sometimes we place ourselves in situations to get offended just because we think we need answers. The answers I received changed my life forever.

Even though I read the Lord's Word every day and pray, I really wanted to know how the Lord was going to punish her for what she was doing. Every time I saw this young lady, my heart turned cold and disposition changed to hatred. I rolled my eyes at her and looked her up and down. I wanted her to know I did not like her. I wanted to intimidate her. I wanted her to pay for the pain she was causing me and my family.

My spirit was vexed and heavy because I knew I had not completely turned this situation over to the Lord because I was depressed, anxious and annoyed most of the time. I felt stuck and needed the Lord to help me be free of these emotions. He said forgive her and you will be free. Needless to say, I didn't immediately say yes to His will or way. It seems like every time I wish others would change, the Lord says "you first." Three years later, my words matched up with my heart and the arduous process of forgiving her accelerated. This was very difficult because I didn't want her to think she was getting away with hurting me. But I needed to be healed so I could release myself from this self-imposed prison of unforgiveness.

Despite what I was going through, I knew the Lord had a purpose for allowing it. I desired to go higher in the Lord but wasn't willing to let my flesh go a little lower. I said Lord I am willing to go through the process of forgiving her. He started honoring my requests by placing me in circumstances with this young lady over and over again. Every time I turned around there she was and I was forced to examine my heart and ask myself some tough questions about what I was feeling. Was I really being committed to releasing my pain to the Lord? Then I started praying and asking the Lord to show me this young lady through His eyes. Eventually, I started seeing her as someone who was insecure, self-destructive, possibly victimized as a child and struggles with sin, just like I do.

It is impossible to live in peace if you don't know anything about humility. I can now stand side by side with that young lady, hold a conversation, support her in her endeavors and not be bitter. I am still a work in progress and take no credit for the change occurring on the inside of me. I give all praise and glory to the Lord because I am more effective as a school counselor and mental health counselor where others can share their greatest pains and offenses with me without fear of judgment or bias. The minute you bless someone who harmed you, you break the power of the enemy and open up the door for the Lord to bless you. "Resentment is like drinking poison and then hoping it will kill your enemies." Nelson Mandela

Scripture

"For the Word that God speaks is alive
and full of power; it is sharper than any
two-edged sword, penetrating to the
dividing line of the breath of life (soul) and
(the immortal) spirit, and of joints and marrows
(of the deepest parts of our nature), exposing
and sifting and analyzing and judging the very
thoughts and purposes of the heart."

Hebrews 4:12

CHAPTER THIRTY-TWO
Self-Loathing

I don't feel like being strong. I feel like being a victim of my circumstances. Knowledge about what this particular mindset does to my psyche isn't enough to push past self-defeat. I hate that I feel so inadequate about my abilities. I wish I had enough energy to encourage myself during these times of self-loathing. I feel so undesirable, unloved, and inadequate. How do I get to a place where I can consistently believe in my ability, believe in my qualities, and believe in my self-worth? It is so hard to feel your love and value for me, Lord.

I hear myself saying to myself that everyone else has it better than me. She has a husband who loves her, I'm divorced. She dresses like a million dollars, I rerun my clothes. She makes six figures, I struggle financially. She's very confident and I'm insecure. She is so well spoken, I trip over my words. She has a bubbly personality and can mix and mingle in any crowd, I get anxious and withdraw. She doesn't struggle with what others think about her, I am too darn focused on what others think about me. I really hate how I pick myself apart and have such a difficult time encouraging myself.

I made a promise to myself that on difficult days that I will try to motivate myself out of my self-imposed pit of lies and self defeat. As I type this, I'm currently feeling insecure about my future but I choose to speak the truth about who I truly am. It is impossible to believe I am fearfully and wonderfully made by the Lord if I'm speaking negative things into my life. I choose to say I am victorious, I am loved, I am valuable, I am unique, I am wonderfully made, I am smart, I am beautiful, I am intelligent, I am a loving and caring person, I am successful, I am God's child. I don't have to be like others in order to be worthy. I am already worthy. The Lord has a purpose for my life. It's not her purpose nor his purpose, it's the purpose God has for me. I am unique and have something to give to others that no one else can. Despite what I've gone through, I know those things do not have the final say in who I am. Yes, I was bruised and hurt, but I am healed and do not have to walk in the lies others have told me when I was young. I am awesome! I embrace the truth of who I am. I love me today and so does God forever!

Scripture

"I praise you because I am fearfully
and wonderfully made; your works are wonderful,
I know that full well."

Psalm 139:14

CHAPTER THIRTY-THREE
Just Enough

While my children were growing up, their father and I believed in chores. If I came home in the evening and the chores weren't done, they knew they would hear my mouth and usually couldn't go outside until it was completed. I remember on a few occasions, I would examine their bedrooms and see a bed made with lumps under the quilt, or I would examine the bathroom and see the sink clean but a dirty tub, or I would examine the kitchen and the dishes would be washed but the floor wasn't swept, or I would examine the living room and see half of the furniture polished. My kids did just enough to keep me from complaining. Sometimes I would overlook their "just enough" effort because either I was too tired to be bothered or I got tired of hearing myself say the same words over and over again that didn't seem to make a difference in their lack of effort.

As I think about those years, I take responsibility for partially teaching them to give a "just enough" effort. They knew, from my words, that if they didn't do their chores, they wouldn't get what they wanted. And at times you don't want to complain about everything. Some things you just let slide and you don't make a big deal about it because no one's perfect, right? There are times when I don't feel like giving a 100% effort at home, on my job and even in my relationships. So it's okay, right? But the question is "where does one draw the line when it comes to others giving you a 'just enough' effort"?

My grandmother (a/k/a mom) raised my brother and me some years after our mother died. When we challenged her boundaries, she would say "don't think you are going to give me your butt to kiss." For a long time, I didn't know what that figure of speech meant, but I knew what it meant. If I choose to challenge her authority, I knew there were consequences to be had. My grandmother was nobody's joke! She was five feet even and tough as nails. She said what she meant and meant what she said. And then I think about me – do I mean what I say and say what I mean?

I think about the many times I said to an ex-boyfriend, you better "show and prove, or get the boot" (lyrics by Erykah Badu in *Call Tyrone*). They would listen intently and acknowledge what my heart was saying and agree to give me what I needed in order to stay in this relationship. It felt good being heard. I knew things would change because their promises were really convincing. But just like Christopher Williams said in his 1989 song "Promises Promises we don't keep; promises promises, we can't eat or sleep." In other words, "action speaks louder than words." They would give me just enough to keep me quiet.

So the question is "how can you get a person to change—to consistently give you more, love you more, respect you more, and treat you the way you want to be treated?" The answer is, plain and simple, you can't. My complaints and pleas weren't enough to get him to action. I thought his lack of action was a reflection of who I was. I thought "is it me, am I the one with the problem?" The only person that can change him, is him. I learned after many years, I cannot make anyone do something they don't have it in their heart to do. The only person I am in control of changing, is me! I had to ask myself "is just enough, really enough?" Not if I want more for my life.

I thank God I had the courage to take a hard, long look at why I thought just enough was enough for such a long time. I compromised what my heart was telling me to do. I knew I deserved to be loved, but it had to start with me, loving me, and not settling for the "okie doke." When a relationship ends, it usually means that someone is maturing. And that individual is now ready to have more than the relationship offers. (Iyanla Vanzant) I am now ready to be loved, honored, and treated the way I really want to be treated.

Scripture

"But seek first his kingdom and his righteousness,
and all these things will be given to you as well."

Matthew 6:33

CHAPTER THIRTY-FOUR

Let Go, Let God?

I find myself wondering if I had seized every opportunity while he was growing up to educate and equip him for the unexpected things in life. Could I have sat down a little longer to find out what was on his mind? Could I have reached out to him instead of continuing to talk on the telephone or watching television when I had this sense that something wasn't quite right? Could I have educated myself more about what teens and pre-adults go through instead of playing the guessing game and ignoring the obvious signs (the signs that are evident today in his personality which are lingering affects of my lack of attention).

What can I do now to save my son? He's remorseful that he committed that crime. As a mother, I know he made those choices because he didn't care about his life. He went through so many changes which caused him hurt and anger. He loved college but unfortunately had to leave after one year of studies, he lost his great-grandmother to cancer, and his dad and I separated after 23 years of marriage. All of this occurred in one year's time. These changes shook his foundation and he dealt with it badly. Hell, I dealt with it badly. My son, my firstborn son, how can I save your life?

I pleaded with the judge for a lesser sentence and explained all of the losses our family had experienced. As I waited for the judge to speak, I prayed and pleaded with the Lord to save my son, my firstborn son's life. As I sat there, my mind drifted to all the times his dad and I were inconsistent with his consequences and didn't follow through. I thought about all those times when he struggled in grade school and we didn't get him the proper tutoring. I thought about all those times when he cried out, by way of his actions, and we thought "that's what boys do." I think about those times with much regret and sorrow. Please don't take my son, my firstborn son from me. Why Lord why does he have to go away? Why does it have to be for this length of time? I cried out "Be merciful to me, O LORD, for I am in distress; my eyes grow weak with sorrow, my soul and my body with grief." (Psalm 31:9)

I'm so mad at you Lord for allowing all of these losses and pain to occur in our lives like a domino effect. What is it that you're trying to say Lord? I hope I'm ready to receive it. Then the Lord said, "I need your son's full, undivided attention, and you are in the way. Every time he has been into trouble, you rescued him. Every time he complained about not getting his way, you gave in. Every time something occurred monetarily, you paid his way. He needs to learn how to depend upon me for his needs, not you. You are an enabler and a rescuer. How can he appreciate the treasure found in the toils and joys of adulthood if you refuse to let him grow up? I realize you want to save him from pain, but pain brings gain, growth, stamina and strength. Your involvement deprives him of that. Let Go and Let God!"

Oh how difficult it was to let go. But I didn't have any other choice because my son was away. Despite not knowing every right decision to make while he was growing up, I know he wouldn't be the man he is today if it had not been for his time away. You love the Lord, you are a devoted, attentive father, a caring uncle, loving son and man with an impeccable work ethic and drive for success. I thank God I finally let go and let God.

The Lord saved my son, my firstborn son's life.

Scripture

I was young and now I am old,
yet I have never seen the righteous forsaken
or their children begging bread.

Psalm 37:25

CHAPTER THIRTY-FIVE

My Person

She's a nuisance, bossy, opinionated, wise, stubborn, confidant, tolerant and loving. She's my person. She knows my sorrows, expectations for life, hurts, joys and temptations. She's my person. She shares her struggles and at the end of her words, she praises the Lord. She's my person. She's not intimated by my fits when she gives me her honest opinion about what I should or shouldn't have done. She's my person. She's my prayer partner.

I didn't always have that type of person in my life consistently who didn't mind stepping in my mess and helping me out. I remember being in messes and friends feeding me the words that usually kept me in my mess and then talking about my messes with others who had similar messes. For me, there were so few friends that I could expose my heart to without fearing they would judge me or gossip with their friends or spouses. Some females who knew I was struggling would call me just to get the information. I felt they did this so they could gloat about my trouble not being their trouble. I knew they were this type of person because they gossiped about most of their friends to me. You can't trust everyone with your secrets. Learning this lesson came at a great price.

My cousin Cindy shared with me her experience with her prayer partners of over ten years back in 2002. I was in awe because I could never imagine being this transparent let alone sticking with a commitment for that length of time (Monday through Friday, for ten years). However, I knew I needed that type of person in my life that would hold my confidences, hold me accountable, and not be envious of my achievements and non-judgmental. I needed that person who wasn't so quick to give me her opinion or throw Bible verses in my face about why I shouldn't have done what I did. Finding that person to share my issues with needed to be done with wisdom and after much prayer.

It is a blessing and privilege to be able to find that person, who you know in your heart, you can share your ugliest of habits with and her response is nonchalant and encourages you that it won't always be like this.

Do you have that person? That someone who you know is always praying for you about your unChrist-like thoughts, your foolish choices, or your temptations. That someone whom you can share things with without trepidation? Be wise in your selection and ask the Lord to reveal her/him to you. If He hasn't, wait! Everyone is not ready to shoulder your issues, secrets and blessings. Be wise in your selection and ask the Lord for Wisdom. Proverbs 4:7 states "Wisdom is supreme; therefore get wisdom. Though it cost all you have, get understanding." Wisdom always leads to God's best for your life.

I thank God for showing me in December 2002 who my prayer partner for life was. I love you Enette. You are "My Person."

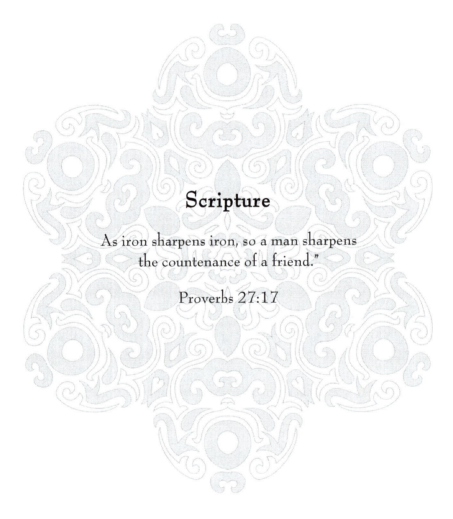

Scripture

As iron sharpens iron, so a man sharpens
the countenance of a friend."

Proverbs 27:17

CHAPTER THIRTY-SIX

Elephant in the Room

My dad was telling me a story about rubbing my stepmother's feet with healing oils because they were tired and swollen. While telling the story, he laughed and I could tell he felt proud of what he had done. I laughed along and felt particularly delighted for him and how he was caring for his wife. At that moment, my mind drifted to a time in my life when I didn't feel so proud of him.

Some time ago, while visiting my father's home, they were sharing a story from the late 1960s about what happened after a party one evening. While walking home, they were a little tipsy and hungry and bought two rib sandwiches. They couldn't wait to get home and gobble them down. When they walked up the hallway, they heard Mitsy, their German shepherd barking. They opened the door to a wagging tale happy dog, put the bag of food on the stove and proceeded to freshen up and change their clothes. When dad returned to the kitchen, he called out to my stepmom inquiring about where she put the rib sandwiches. My stepmom came out of the bathroom and said she put them on the stove. They both frantically searched for the food. Then all of a sudden, they both froze and looked at the dog. Mitsy was licking her lips and looked guilty. They couldn't believe and was furious at the same time that the dog ate their sandwiches along with the bag and aluminum foil. We all laughed so hard at the story. But then I became silent because that event was in the late 1960s and I thought "where was I?" That was during the time when dad and my mother were separated. He was reliving the memories of the late 1960s as a happy time but it wasn't a happy time for me. I immediately became irritated. Why weren't they sensitive about what that time meant to me? Why did they think it was okay to share that story with me?

I was immediately sucked back to that time and felt hurt, abandoned, and lonely all over again but this time, I was an adult. I could now make sense of those feelings and was very angry. I told them I had to go and would call when I got home. During the drive home, I fussed and cried because they made me remember, and I thought I had forgotten about that sad time in my life, that time when my mommy died, that time when I felt abandoned, that time when life stood still.

Oprah Winfrey asked author Michael Singer from his book entitled "The Unthethered Soul", how do you know when you've healed from an offense? He said when you bring it up it doesn't hurt anymore. Because I am a reflective, introspective person who will eventually do the hard work to grow as a Godly woman, I knew I had to do some more work with forgiving my father for abandoning us now some 44 years later. I was so mad that I had to revisit this place, this pain. I honestly didn't feel like going there. So I didn't until sometime later when I offended a dear friend and needed her forgiveness. We too tiptoed around the offense and never dealt with it. We are no longer friends.

When you refuse to talk about that elephant in the room, that big huge hurt, you learn to be phony with others, including yourself. I needed to find my authentic self. Lord where is she, who is she, help me find her.

For a long time, I didn't have a relationship with my father. There were many unspoken hurts and pains within our relationship but I thank God for healing our wounds. We are very close now and can talk about anything. I call my father "my stalker-daddy" because if I don't return his call, he will call my kids or drive to my house looking for me. I thank God for healing old wounds. Mommy would be so proud of you, daddy! You're my hero!

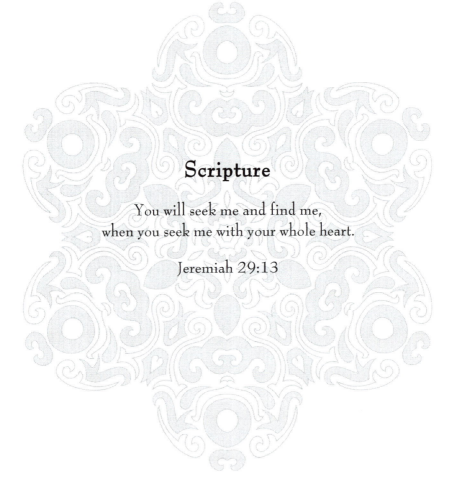

Scripture

You will seek me and find me,
when you seek me with your whole heart.

Jeremiah 29:13

CHAPTER THIRTY-SEVEN

Where Are You?

I search for you but cannot find you. I see your face and recognize your voice but my soul cannot find you? We used to be close. We used to play up and down the streets of Queen Lane with Eddie, Freddy and Marie. Remember those times, remember those days? We were siblings. Life was so simple. Remember during the winter when we didn't own a sled and we made one out of cardboard boxes? I still have the scar on my knee to prove it. We were just kids, playing with other kids, hating to be forced to eat our vegetables. Remember when I got a beating for the trash can you set on fire? You lied and told mommy it was me, and they believed you. That was so wrong, Tony. But we were kids, right? Where are you brother? I see your face and recognize your voice but my soul cannot find you?

What did life do to us early on in our childhood? Did it strip of us our innocence and make us numb to our pain? Was it a lack of acknowledging our feelings about our mother's death? I think we are stuck somewhere because when I see you, I don't recognize who you are, even though I see your face and recognize your voice. I want my brother back from 1969, right before things changed. When we talk on the telephone, you always reminisce and say "Andy, remember when mommy was living and this happened or that happened? I'm so sorry you are stuck back there somewhere remembering all the details and I'm sorry I don't remember."

Children who are not allowed to acknowledge their losses, are prone to major serious psychological and physiological problems. Blocked grief affects how children feel and behave. When children are not permitted to grieve in a healthy way, they comfort themselves with other things which can lead to depression, eating disorder, suicidal ideation, addiction, anger, avoidance-like behaviors, to name a few. Unresolved grief as children, grow into adults who have social, personal, relationship, family, money and health problems. (Gerlach, Break the Cycle) Yes brother, we both have issues!

Adults please remember your children when tragedy or death befalls a family. When you experience pain and sorrow, they experience pain and sorrow too but only through eyes that cannot comprehend coupled with mixed emotions. My brother's and my lack of expressing ourselves about our mother's death and all that occurred growing up, affected our thoughts, belief system and choices up through today. But there's good news. The Lord had a plan for my life (Jeremiah 29:11). And because of the Lord's promises, I trust Him with my life. I know that everything I have gone through, there's a reason for it all. I don't understand why but I trust God that He is working everything out for my good (Romans 8:28). It doesn't make sense at times but I trust God. I still hurt from my losses but I trust God. If it had not been for my losses, abandonment, and abuses, I would not have a heart for people like me. I give to others what I needed growing up and you, my audience, are worth my pain. It took me a long time to see the message in my mess because I spent so much time licking my wounds and rehearsing the pain in my mind. But I thank you Lord for slowly transforming and renewing my mind and heart (Romans 12:2). The Word of God motivates me to change and encourages the insecure places within me. When I'm feeling like a motherless child, the Lord says I am the mother to the motherless (Psalm 68:5). Knowing who we are in Christ will lead us to confident living. Ask the Lord to help you not be a victim of your circumstances but instead to be a victor despite your circumstances.

Scripture

"Therefore I tell you, whatever you ask for
in prayer, believe that you have received it,
and it will be yours."

Mark 11:24

CHAPTER THIRTY-EIGHT
Thief in the Night

Hop scotch, jumping jacks, one two three red light, hide and go seek, and watching the Olympics and mimicking Nadia Comaneci's gymnast moves are a few of my pleasant childhood memories. My grandmother kept my childhood somewhat trouble-free especially after the death of my mother. But caregivers can't always shelter their children from falling prey to other's actions.

I silently screamed please don't touch me like that because it makes me feel so uncomfortable. At age 11, I could not muster the words to make him stop because I was afraid he would be angry with me and I would get in trouble. Today, I can still remember how helpless I felt. I still remember his face, his breath, his hands on me, the taste in his mouth, and his unremorseful expression. I still remember! Why is it so difficult to erase that memory from my childhood? Haven't I gone through enough, Lord? Maybe if I squeeze my eyes shut and grit my teeth hard enough I will forget about you and that day you sexually abused me.

I knew I needed to go for counseling but the therapist is only going to make me think about it, talk about it and remember how I felt. I was in my 20s, 30s and 40s and still remembered. (I need a drink to numb my pain, to erase the memories—if only for a moment.) The therapist told me I was an innocent child, I was the victim and it was not my fault. I thought to myself, "if that is the case, why do I still feel so guilty and ashamed?"

I went through life telling myself it didn't matter and believing that I needed to 'get over it.' But 'getting over it' is only a cliché that works for those who choose to believe the lie and ignore the pain. I knew I hadn't gotten over it because certain events triggered the memories. My therapist reassured me that what I was feeling was absolutely normal because children who are sexually abused quietly suffer from its effects into adulthood. Children who are sexually abused suffer emotional, physical and psychological damage. This damage can cause the victim to be "self-destructive, over-controlling and abusive towards others, as well as addicted to alcohol, drugs, and food and attracted to love partners who abuse them physically, verbally, and emotionally" (Pandora's Closet). As I look back, I can now see how the abuse caused me to exercise so many self-destructive behaviors through my life.

I was tired of walking around with wounds that dictated my present-day thoughts and choices. I wanted to be courageous enough to feel uncomfortable for a moment to work through my emotions. I fervently prayed and asked the Lord to increase my faith (Luke 17:5-6), help my unbelief (Mark 9:24[b]), heal my sin sick soul (Jeremiah 8:22) and to set me free (Psalm 118:5) so I could be used by Him.

As I began my journey of healing, the Lord started showing me how strongholds in my mind will try to keep me from my destiny. The Lord encouraged me to think differently about every situation that was designed to steal my future and separate me from His love (Romans 12:1-2). My abandonment and abuse issues had distorted my thinking when it came to trusting the Lord and others, choosing a companion, walking in my destiny, and my tendency towards self-destructive behaviors. Now I accept where I am as a survivor and gently acknowledge my feelings when my past invades my future. Yes, my history still presents itself today but I am more aware of the strength the Lord has placed in me. If I survived the death of my mother, an absentee father, I can survive this too. I am a survivor in the strength of Jesus. My audience, I am your hope that you can make it through your struggles of sexual abuse. God cares about us and He wants to comfort, heal and make us whole.

Scripture

"Guard my life and rescue me; let me
not be put to shame, for I take refuge in you."

Psalm 25:20

CHAPTER THIRTY-NINE

Silence Within

Whether you are the stepparent or stepchild, the adjustments involved with embracing this new lifestyle can be very challenging. After our mother died, my brother and I were taken out of school and relocated to live with my father, stepmother and baby sister. I felt displaced, unloved and a burden. I felt like I was in a foreign land where I had to learn how to adjust to the moods of this new family. No one taught me how to operate in this new family, no one had a conversation with me about what to expect or what was expected of me.

As a stepchild, I was forced into this lifestyle without my consent or opinion. No introductions, no trial periods, or preconsultations. I was a vulnerable little girl who lost her mother to death one month prior. No one asked me how I felt about my mother's death. In my opinion, over time, their lack of interest led me to believe no one cared. Whenever I brought up the memory of my mother, I felt like that subject was off limits because I would receive snide stares by some or no one would reply to my comments. I learned early in life that the death of my mother and my feelings associated with it were of no significance.

I want to hug that little girl name Andy and tell her I'm sorry she had no one to turn to, and understand her feelings. In the 1960s, kids didn't verbalize their dislikes nor did they talk about their issues. Kids were seen and not heard. This made me feel insignificant and unimportant. I said, "who's this, daddy?" He said, this is your stepmother. I said, "where's my mommy?" I knew she had died but when is she coming back? No answers, just blank stares and then I'm left standing all alone, without consolation. I learned early in life that my feelings didn't matter and no one really cared what I was feeling, and so I learned how to stuff my feelings and pretend that what I was feeling was insignificant.

How do you move from feeling suspicious of others to trusting again? First, the word trust means a "firm belief in the reliability, truth, ability, or strength of someone or something." This seems like a tall order for any human being to fill especially with someone who has developing trust issues. I walked around for years being suspicious of others, waiting for them to disappoint me, cheat on me or leave me. But when you walk around guarded, with a suspicious nature, you have a tendency to look for mistrust in others which only validates your desire to not trust them. And you will eventually find what you're looking for no matter how great or small.

This method of distrusting as a lifestyle is not the life for a child of God. The Lord expects us to trust Him explicitly. We must learn how to exercise His kingdom principles of "bearing all things, believing all things, hoping all things, and enduring all things (1 Corinthians 13:7). You can only do this if you are willing to shed your guarded emotions and release them to the Lord. I believe one of the greatest steps in trusting others is by forgiving them. Once you decide to release your offenders from your bondage of unforgiveness, then that cloud of suspicion begins to clear and you can begin to see the good in people. Remember to always pray and ask the Lord for wisdom and discernment regarding who to trust your heart with.

And lastly, remember, the only person who is totally trustworthy is God. Whenever you feel like someone has hurt you beyond repair just know the Lord sympathizes with all of our infirmities and understands our pain. (Hebrews 4:15). Follow His example of forgiveness (Colossians 3:13). He is waiting to heal you so you can begin to love and trust again.

Scripture

"Trust in the Lord with all your heart,
and lean not to your own understanding.
In all your ways acknowledge Him, and He will
direct your path. Be not wise in your own eyes."

Proverbs 3:5-7

CHAPTER FORTY
Trick or Treat

Everyone knows the phrase "trick or treat." It's about Halloween and kids dressing up, pretending to be someone they are not for a day. I remember neighborhood kids coming to my house and saying the words 'trick or treat.' I would say 'who are you?' They would scream, guess! I would go through the long list of neighborhood kids until I pretended to give up and say, I don't know? They would snatch off their mask and say "it's me Ms. Brown." And I would pretend to be surprised and shout, "I didn't know it was you, you tricked me." As quiet as it was kept, I already knew who they were because I recognized their voices.

This story triggered a memory of an incident that occurred not too long ago. I received a friend request from my Bishop David G. Evans on Facebook. I was totally shocked because I had tried to 'friend' him years prior but his friend's list was filled to capacity. So needless to say, when I received his friend request I was excited. I also had some apprehensions and immediately started going through my pictures to see if I had anything questionable on Facebook because as you all know by now, I struggle from time to time with my need to impress people. I searched for about a minute and then said, I'm a grown woman and have much self-respect.

The next day, my Bishop inboxed me with a prophetic message that left me kind of baffled because it wasn't quite clear in its meaning. I don't do well with reading between the lines and I didn't quite understand what he was trying to say. I read it five times and replied asking if he could be a little more clear about what he was trying to prophesy. There are so many occasions when the Holy Spirit speaks to us about what's a trick or what's a treat. We often push the promptings of the Holy Spirit aside because what we are hearing or reading appeals to our flesh. Bishop's reply left me feeling vexed and condemned. As I reread the message, I said to myself "you're acting like you have no common sense. Pray and ask for discernment." The Lord started showing me the imposter behind the Facebook mask. I was taught by my 'real' Bishop that you cannot move with strength those things you don't understand. Knowledge is power. In other words, knowledge directs our actions and enables us to find the difference between right and wrong, good and bad. Knowledge can help you overcome your weaknesses and faults, and helps you face falsities with courage and confidence. I learned from my Bishop that whenever anyone speaks a prophetic word over your life it must line it up with scripture and then you should watch to see if it comes to past.

The thing that initially troubled me was I believed what the imposter was originally prophesying about me. During a Wednesday night Bible Study, Reverend Smith said "snakes always come with a conversation and a question (Genesis 3:1). Snakes know how to smell weakness on you and usually say what you are already saying to yourself." (Sermon on December 2, 2012) So what was I saying to myself that made me believe the imposter? After much introspection, I realized I was saying that my God does not love me unconditionally because I make mistakes? If I believed that, then I would believe he came to condemn me of my wrongdoing instead of saving me from my many confessed sins (1 John 1:9). The first thing the Lord brought to my attention was I was being accused of not doing something that I have been doing at 5:10 a.m., Monday through Friday, for ten years straight – and that's prayer and reading God's Word with my prayer partner. Don't get me wrong, I can never study and pray enough but I was being made to feel condemned by the one thing I was doing right. I immediately removed the imposter from my friend's list and contacted my church regarding what happened.

I want to challenge you in the area that I fell short. When someone comes to you and shares a prophetic word, will you be quick, like me, to believe it's a treat or will you study (2 Timothy 2:15) to see if it's a trick? I'm learning daily to rightly divide the Word of Truth so I won't be had by the imposter behind the mask.

Scripture

"Beloved, do not believe every spirit, but test the spirits to see whether they are from God, for many false prophets have gone out into the world."

1 John 4:1

CHAPTER FORTY-ONE
Beauty for Ashes

Why couldn't you tell me in person? Why did I have to find out this way? An email message, one Fall evening, changed my life forever. Mom, I have something to tell you, "I'm pregnant."

I felt like the world around me was closing in on me. The news took my breath away. My head was spinning and my mind was racing. This can't be so! This is her first year in college, let alone her first semester. I screamed No! I felt all energy was sucked out of me and all I could do was go to bed. Sleep was nowhere to be found. The only thing I had were my thoughts. "I should have put that child on the pill. Oh my God, what are the church folks going to say." Oh my God no, why is this happening again, me at 17 years old – my life and pregnancy all over again in my face to remember? Why is life repeating itself? And then I started to condemn myself. "I didn't prepare her for college-life. Why didn't I put her on the pill like my cousins told me? I know they're going to say "I told you so." What are people going to say about our well put together family? Our image, from what I believed, was impeccable. And then out of desperation I thought, maybe she can get an abortion. But then I was so mad that I remembered how adamant I was against abortion. Desperation will make you compromise and sell your soul for a way out. I was crushed.

When Colleen came home, I couldn't look her straight in the eyes. I was so disappointed but more so embarrassed about what other people were going to say. And I was also more afraid of getting in return what I had given others whose sins had been exposed for the world to see — no compassion and judgmentalism. Then the Lord asked me "how did others treat you when you got pregnant at 17 years old? Wow, that was a loaded question which I didn't want to go back in history to answer.

It was September of 1978, when I found out I was pregnant by my high school boyfriend. I remember pleading with the Lord "please take this away and I will never have sex again." I felt like I wanted to die. I remembered the disgusting look on my father's face, as he shook his head side to side. I think I remember being in the back seat of his car and looking at him through the rear view mirror. I felt so bad, like I was the only person in the world who had every gotten pregnant in high school. My grandmother was so disgusted with me that she couldn't even look at me. My family whispered behind my back while I was in the other room, but I could hear them. Why did mom have to invite them over anyway? Like I was on display. And I remember my grandmother saying "you better not tell anyone in the church. Keep your mouth shut." I felt so ashamed and unworthy of forgiveness, so I didn't ask for it, and then got a pompous attitude about the whole thing and started to rebel. I subconsciously thought if I'm that disgusting, then I might as well act like it. I felt like no one was in my corner, no one hugged me and said "Andy, we all make mistakes. God still loves you and so do I. We will get through this together" But those words never came to me.

Fast forward to 2002. My baby girl was me, and I gripped my heart in sorrow because I was projecting what others did to me on to her. I didn't want her to feel what I felt in 1978. I sat down with her and cried with her and held her. She was me and I wanted to give her what I so desperately needed in 1978.

"You intended to harm me, but God intended it for good to accomplish what is now being done, the saving of many lives." (Genesis 50:20) When God gets involved, He takes what Satan meant to destroy us and turns it so that it works for our good instead. How did Colleen getting pregnant work for our good? In many ways, I became a more compassionate person but most importantly, that next year, the Lord saw fit to take home my mom (grandmom) four months after Julian was born. Her death in 2003 almost destroyed me. But there was a ram in the bush and his name was Julian. The Lord can take any negative situation, and through His miracle-working power use it to make us stronger and useful for helping His people through the challenges of their lives. I thank God for teaching me how to love and forgive regardless of our mistakes.

Scripture

"To grant to those who mourn in Zion, to give them
an ornament of beauty instead of ashes, the oil of joy
instead of mourning, the garment of praise instead
of a heavy, burdened and failing spirit that they
may be called oaks of righteousness the planting
of the Lord, that He may be glorified."

Isaiah 61:3

CHAPTER FORTY-TWO

Prayer Changes Hearts

Do you know what it feels like when your boss wants to get rid of you for no apparent reason? It seemed like everything I did was never good enough for him. He just wanted me out. I'm not sure if he wanted to replace me with someone else but whatever the reason, he made it clear that he did not want me working for him. I would get reprimanded for not being at my desk when he asked me to run an errand for him. He would walk by me in the morning, and would not acknowledge me. It seemed he was trying to make me miserable so I would quit. Once he blamed me for botching up a project that I didn't work on. He was furious with me. I explained that I didn't work on that particular project and his response was that I should have worked on that project and that's why it needs to be done again. I had to work overtime fixing someone else's mistakes. I felt like I couldn't do anything to please him no matter how hard I tried. I thought about going to human resources to complain until someone informed me his family member worked in that department. My father always told me to never quit a job unless you had another one lined up. But Lord knows, I was on the verge of quitting with no replacement job in sight.

During lunchtime each day, I met with a few coworkers for Bible Study and prayer. I shared my concerns with them and we started praying for my boss. For six months straight, we prayed for him constantly. I started interviewing for other jobs but no one seemed to be hiring. I felt stuck and miserable. It's a bad feeling when you dread going to work. I started dreading Sunday evenings because I knew the next day I had to work. I started to hate my job and felt tempted to call out often just so I didn't have to deal with his ridicule. His treatment towards me was so obvious that other coworkers started noticing.

While praying for my boss, I started noticing my dislike towards him change to compassion. I cannot explain it but I know the Lord was doing a work in my heart. I started seeing my boss as an unhappy man whose life was in need of a Savior. No one who acts like this inside can be happy with themselves. I started exercising Mark 12:31 – loving my neighbor as myself. It was not easy but I needed to believe that my God is a God of justice and would make things right. I knew I could not handle this situation in my own power. This conflict had to be handled "not by might, nor by power but by the Spirit sayeth the Lord." Zechariah 4:6

The following week, my boss was absent for three days. When he arrived on Thursday, his right arm was broken and in a cast. He had fallen off of his bicycle while in a marathon. He needed my assistance with many tasks including buttoning his shirt sleeve. The following week while I was buttoning his sleeve, he said, "I don't know what I would do without you. Thank you for being so patient with me."

Wow, look at God! Whenever you pray to the Lord for a change in someone, oftentimes He is waiting for the change to begin in you. My circumstances didn't change until my heart changed towards my boss. The Holy Spirit gave me the power to carry out His plans no matter how difficult the journey. When you pray, the Lord releases His power so that our actions glorify Him and demonstrate to others that He is able to change the hardest of hearts.

134

Scripture

"Repay no one evil for evil, but take thought
for what is honest and proper and noble in
the sight of everyone. If possible, as far as it depends
on you, live at peace with everyone. Beloved,
never avenge yourselves, but leave the way open for
[God's] wrath; for it is written, Vengeance is Mine,
I will repay, says the Lord. But if your enemy is
hungry, feed him; if he is thirsty, give him drink; for
by so doing you will heap burning coals upon
his head. Do not let yourself be overcome by evil,
but overcome (master) evil with good."

Romans 12:17-21

CHAPTER FORTY-THREE

In the Meantime

I miss my mom (grandmom) so much. I'm not sure if I go through missing her the same time each year but I think it's more so during significant shifts in my life that either cause me challenges or blessings. I believe me needing her to celebrate with or support me is what I miss the most. You never ever get over missing your mother. It's been 10 years and two months since her passing but it feels just like yesterday. I remember the last time I laid on her lap, at 42 years old. She would scratch my back. I usually laid on her lap when she was on the telephone because I knew the back scratch would be as long as she was on the telephone, which was usually up to an hour. At times during her telephone call, she would pause and stop scratching my back. That's when I would shake my body and make a grunt to signal her to continue. I think those moments were cute and precious.

I've been praying since mom's passing that the Lord would connect me with an elderly Christian lady who would call and see about me. I prayed that she would take an interest in my life and my children's and grand's lives. I prayed she would come to my home and sit and chit chat. I prayed she would surprise me with movie outings and dinner at the diner. I prayed she would call me because she would sense something wasn't quite right with me. I prayed I would confide in her my deepest of troubles without judgment. I pray for her often and she's nowhere to be found.

Lord why are some of my prayers answered and others not? Lord you know my heart's desire but my answer seem nowhere to be found. Why would something like this be so difficult? I'm just asking for an elderly Christian to come and see about me and make me feel that I matter. The Lord spoke to my weeping heart and said "give to others what you want to receive. I may not decide that this is My Will for your life but in the meantime, give the love you have stored up for your elderly mother and give to the children who are motherless. Give the love you have stored up for the woman who cries in the midnight hour over their losses. Give to the husband and wife whose marriage is strained due to breaches of trust. Give to the stranger you cross in the store whose life is lonely. Give to others what you want so desperately. Your giving will be returned to you in due time. In the meantime, give what you so desperately want."

Scripture

Give, and it will be given to you. A good measure, pressed down, shaken together and running over, will be poured into your lap. For with the measure you use, it will be measured to you."

Luke 6:38

CHAPTER FORTY-FOUR

If I Were You, I Would . . . .

Friends and family have shared their opinion about what they believe I should do with my life, particularly surrounding the time of my divorce. I believe many shared their advice with no harm intended however, some opinions shared appeared to be self-seeking. Several individuals approached me saying if I were you I would wait to divorce for at least two years. Others said if I were you I would not date until two years after my divorce. A few said if I were you I wouldn't get divorced because God hates divorce. And some said they would support me in whatever decision I choose to make for my life. Since hindsight is 20/20, I would now agree with some of the opinions I thought were self-seeking and would disagree with some opinions I thought were good. But I was emotionally and spiritually in a different place during that time. For 23 years, I didn't know anything else but marriage. Now I am in this new place and I'm trying to get to know who I am as a single Christian woman.

One thing that intrigued me about this 'if I were you I would' situation was why did others feel free to make such statements to me? I believe one reason was that I had become emotionally dependent on others. Emotional dependency is partly our need to depend on others to give us our self-image. As a result of feeling abandoned at a young age coupled with being afraid to express my emotions, I grew up with a fractured self-image. Those with a fractured self-image lack confidence which causes them to fear anything new. I realized I first believed this lie when my mother died when I was 7 years old, later to be separated from my father at the age of 9 years old. It is normal for children who are raised with chronic losses to take on incredible fear and feelings of failure. I learned to look to others to have the right answers because I doubted myself and was afraid of failure.

I still occasionally struggle with being emotionally dependent on others because I was accustomed to seeking their advice and approval. In my quest to live under the umbrella of what others thought I should do with my life, I lost my sense of independence and my responsibility to take care of myself. I taught them that they knew what was best for me. And by creating that type of relationship, I gave them permission to continue to guide the choices I needed to make for my life.

The one thing I love about the Word of God is that He speaks directly to your circumstances. It might not speak specifically to your particular situation, but there's truth in His Word and all you have to do is pray about it and ask the Holy Spirit to help you rightfully divide the Word of truth. In 2 Corinthians 10:12, the apostle Paul talks about those who compare themselves to others as being unwise and without understanding. When you depend on others for the answers you lack confidence in your own gifting. I desired a ministry where I encourage hurting people to strive to their fullest potential despite their circumstances. But how can I do this if I am insecure? The Lord has given each one of us an assignment and the ability to accomplish it. You cannot successful do this if you are constantly second guessing who the Lord created you to be. If you believe the Word of God, then you should believe you are fearfully and wonderfully made (Psalm 139:14). Get busy living out God's purpose for your life.

Scripture

"So do not throw away your confidence; it will be
richly rewarded. You need to persevere
so that when you have done the will of God,
you will receive what he has promised."

Hebrews 10:35-36

CHAPTER FORTY-FIVE

Mental Clutter

W hen I think of clutter, I think of a collection of things lying about in an untidy form. The examples that come to mind are rooms, desks, drawers or a car's trunk. I realize I have hoarder-like tendencies so I am no stranger to clutter. But one example I think is worthy of mention is our mind. Can our minds be filled with clutter as well? If clutter is a collection of things, is it possible for our minds to have a collection of jumbled non-productive thoughts, also known as mental clutter?

I unfortunately had an experience with a dear friend who made accusations about me. Needless to say, it was very hurtful and difficult to move past. All I could think and talk about were his words and tone. I tried to get his accusations out of my mind but the more I thought about it, the more I talked about it. I called my prayer partner and several close friends and shared the story each time with them, with the same emotion. The more I recounted the details, the angrier I became. My mind was consumed with mental clutter.

How does one begin to clean out mental clutter? I honestly didn't want to stop thinking about his offense because I believed I had a right to stay angry. If I gave up my right to be angry, then I felt like I was sending a message that what he did was okay. And it wasn't okay. But the other side of me realized that there should be a balance between being angry and mulling over a grievance which is a form of sin. (Ephesians 4:26). I knew I needed to allow myself time to process my feelings but I also knew I needed to press past persistent unforgiveness which had the potential to turn into bitterness. When your spirit, mind and soul are full of unforgiveness, you cannot grow spiritually. You stumble and stop making progress. (Joyce Meyers)

I realized I've wasted so much time in the past being angry at this person or that person for years and years. It didn't do me a bit of good harboring unforgiveness. I needed to control my emotions and not let my emotions control me. It was a choice I needed to make. Once I made the choice to stop talking about the offense and start thinking about other things, I started to feel less burdened by what happened. As I am working through my pain, my mind might occasionally frequent that place of being offended because I'm human. However, I do have a choice of how long I'm going to stay there or whether I'm going to go at all. I choose this moment to fill my mind with thoughts of what is true, noble, right, pure, love and admirable. Philippians 4:8

Once I decided to exercise this scripture for my life, the Lord told me to bless my offender. WHAT! See the Lord always has to take it a step further. Isn't choosing to think on things that are of good report enough? It's interesting how the Lord allows you to take baby steps of forgiveness and then says now I need you to take a leap of faith and be a blessing. I needed to mature and stretch a little more. I didn't honor the Lord's request right away because my flesh needed a few days to think about whether what I was hearing was the Lord or the enemy. That's called doubt. I didn't want to take the chance on blessing him and he not appreciate how difficult it was for me to even bless him. The Lord said it is not your job to control your offender's response. It is only your job to be obedient to Me!

I don't know how my offender felt after I blessed him but I know the Lord is working everything out for my good and His glory. Choosing to apply scripture in my life during challenging times has proven over and over again to be an effective tool to gaining peace. Thank you Lord for helping me get rid of my mental clutter.

Scripture

Do not be overcome by evil,
but overcome evil with good.

Romans 12:21

CHAPTER FORTY-SIX

Under New Management

L iving a life where you have been afraid to say no to others feels so restricting and downright frustrating. I dread it when others ask for a favor because I know there's a possibility that I'm going to be confronted with the agony of contemplating a 'no' answer. When contemplation begins, anxiety builds within me and it increases when I think about actually following through with saying no. I begin to scratch my head, breathe deeply, wring my hands and pace. I hate putting myself through this. It's unfortunate that giving into others eases my anxiety while at the same time wells-up self-hatred.

Where did I learn that giving into others' requests was a better choice than standing up for my own choices? Where did I learn that it was okay to appease the whims of others while at the same time degrading my choice, my voice? Was it because I was unknowingly harassed as a child by others to keep my feelings to myself, to keep my mouth shut, to be seen and not heard? These messages were repeatedly acted out by others throughout my childhood (after the death of my mother) and eventually I believed them. And now this child is an adult with a child-like (dependent) belief system.

This type of thinking is a form of imprisonment. Your freedom to choose is voluntarily being held captive by others. When you are imprisoned in your thinking someone else holds the keys and is in control of your freedom of expression. You silently fight to unshackle the chains but every time you open your mouth to say your truth, your fear paralyzes your heart and your lies continue to live and gains strength for tomorrow.

How do you find the balance between your 'yes' and your 'no'? The answer is by living in the truth of who you are. I refuse to go into another year wasting my mind on the opinions of others. I desire a new perspective and a new way of looking at my situation and circumstances. I need my mind ready for my future blessings and victories. You must believe you are fearfully and wonderfully made (Psalm 139:14) and you are the head and not the tail (Deuteronomy 28:13). You were not created to be anybody's puppet, anybody's fool or anybody's jump-off. You live according to the opinions of others when you don't believe the truth of what the Word of God says concerning you. You choose to dumb-down your authentic Godly self by living under the shadow of others. It is a choice. And no matter how difficult it is to reprogram your thinking, don't you think you're worth it? What you say to yourself gives birth to your belief system and actions. Start saying the right thing to yourself and the right response will follow. If you are truly interested in connecting with your authentic self, then do the work to figure out why you are not satisfied with the decisions that you are making for your life. Aren't you ready to get your mind prepared for your future blessings and victories? It is with the mind that we serve the Lord (Isaiah 26:3). You need to have a mind to change from all the poison that is hindering you from what God is about to pour into your life. Unshackle the chains from your past and speak your truth in love.

146

Scripture

"Do not conform any longer to the pattern of this world, but be transformed by the renewing of your mind. Then you will be able to test and approve what God's will is—his good, pleasing and perfect will."

Romans 12:2

CHAPTER FORTY-SEVEN

Migraine-ville

I've never had migraines before and now I'm going on four weeks and haven't missed a day. I've spent two days in the hospital and four days out of work. I'm not used to being incapacitated like this. Life, at times, comes to a stand-still because the migraines are paralyzing and force me to lie down. I am a very busy person and have many things to do. I also am a person who always has food in the refrigerator and my home is, for the most party, tidy. But at this very moment, my cupboard is bare and almost every room in my home is unkempt. I am at a place in my life where I find myself once again vacationing in Migraine-ville.

Migraine-ville is a resort for those whose hectic lifestyles are comprised of overloaded schedules, diminished energy level, a poor diet, lack of exercise, acres of stress, dysfunctional relationships, people pleasing and sparse time with the Lord. This AAA, Four Diamond, all-Preferred Club resort offers its vacationers a spiritual, tranquil, loving, and restful getaway. This getaway is only for the experienced-seeking traveler who is well qualified. This resort has an oceanfront view of Heaven, endless prayer time, hours of rest, agenda-less activities, quiet time for the Lord to speak and a new outlook for your spiritual life. A stunning view awaits you. So unwind, relax and pamper yourself with one of the many, well-deserved treatments. Make your special time unforgettable.

While visiting Migraine-ville, I learned many valuable lessons. This resort forced me into quiet solitude with the Lord to teach me how out-of-control my life was. While in Migraine-ville, it was difficult for me to relax because I tried to control this time with being busy. But the migraine intensified when I exposed myself too soon to movement, light and noise. Migraine-ville taught me about self-care. My stress level was largely due to a lack of rest, meditation, exercise and quality time with the Lord. While in Migraine-ville, I enjoyed basking in the presence of the Lord for relief and direction. The Lord needed me to be still so He could reveal the purpose of my next journey. The Lord revealed that I was uncomfortable with being still because I wasn't ready to connect with my issues. Busyness clouded my thoughts about my issues. That place was too painful to encounter so I stayed away by being busy. However, the Lord's desire for this next chapter in my life was for me to connect with the issues, pains and habits which stemmed from my childhood. This next journey was going to be a time of pruning and the Lord used Migraine-ville to reveal that my busyness gave me an excuse to not do a lot of the other things He commanded me to do.

Periodically, I forget about my vacation time in Migraine-ville and find myself getting busy once again until my vision gets spotted which signals the onset of a migraine. It's at that moment I plead with the Lord to not take me back to Migraine-ville if I promised to slow down and spend more quality time with Him. Thank God, it's been 10 months since my last vacation in Migraine-ville. Make the necessary adjustments before the Lord creates a vacation spot for you.

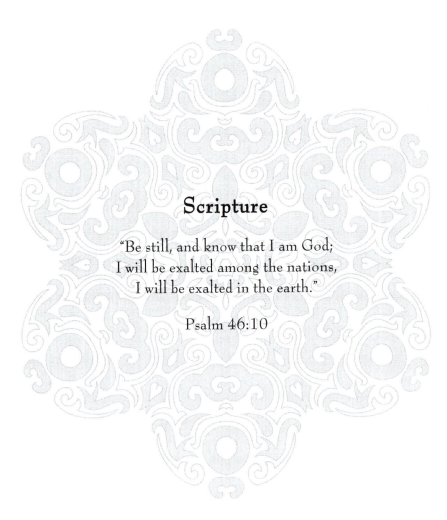

Scripture

"Be still, and know that I am God;
I will be exalted among the nations,
I will be exalted in the earth."

Psalm 46:10

CHAPTER FORTY-EIGHT

Mr. Parking Garage

I couldn't wait to get off the expressway. Why am I getting caught at so many lights? He cut me off on purpose. Get out of my way! Finally, I'm pulling in the parking garage and there he is. Mr. Parking Garage. When he spoke, his voice brightened up my day. He asked me if anyone had ever told me that my hands were beautiful. I'd never heard that compliment before. He said I hope your significant other appreciates your beautiful hands. I giggled in a high school girlish type of way and parked my car. When I got out, he always noticed what I wore. He said oh you have on blue today. You wore brown yesterday. I like the blue. I smiled and walked in the direction of my job. As I turned around, he was smiling and I returned a soft smile too. I couldn't think about anything else all day but his compliment and smile. Coworkers asked why I was so cheerful. They assumed it was my significant other. Each day I carefully picked out my clothes and made sure my hands were not dry. I put on perfume and made sure my make-up was flawless. I had to look good for Mr. Parking Garage.

Temptation is an unexpected tornado that can catch you unaware. What seems like something mildly innocent has the potential of turning into a severe storm. But I was just like many individuals who think that flirting is no big deal and you can handle it. When you're married, you have a tendency to take one another for granted and not notice each other like before. This man was noticing me in ways my significant other wasn't and it got my attention to the point that I was taking extra time in the morning to look good for him, Mr. Parking Garage.

I started to feel convicted about my behavior but not enough to not desire the attention. I decided to ask the Lord to help me not look forward to seeing Mr. Parking Garage every morning. I asked the Lord to help me not think about him at all. I asked the Lord to help me even though my flesh still desired the attention.

Two weeks later, I drove to the parking garage and he wasn't there. I thought he must be out sick. The next day, no Mr. Parking Garage. And the next day, he wasn't there again. I became concerned and asked the new attendant where he was. He said he was transferred to another location. I was shocked and loudly exclaimed, "why?" The attendant said he wasn't sure. As I walked away disappointed, I couldn't help but chuckle at the Lord and how he intervened. Even though my flesh was disappointed my Spirit was elated because my attraction to another man was a stumbling block.

As long as you let your flesh rule your decisions, you are never free. (Galatians 5:1) My mind and my will were telling me what I wanted and not telling me anything about what God wanted. Receiving attention made me feel validated and special, and my only validation should come from the Lord. The encounter with Mr. Parking Garage taught me a valuable lesson about not putting confidence in the flesh. (Philippians 3:3) I thought I could handle that little innocent flirting but take heed less you fall. I pray every morning for the Lord to keep my flesh in check, in all areas of my life, so I don't fall victim to the enemy.

Scripture

"So, if you think you are standing firm,
be careful that you don't fall! No temptation has
seized you except what is common to man.
And God is faithful; he will not let you be
tempted beyond what you can bear. But when you
are tempted, he will also provide a way out so
that you can stand up under it."

1 Corinthians 10:12-13

CHAPTER FORTY-NINE

Prognosis

P salm 100:4, Philippians 4:6-7 and Philippians 4:11-13: These are the scriptures I recited silently to myself as I waited six hours for the doctors to begin my surgery. In my human nature, I wanted to fuss about how much time I was waiting particularly on an empty stomach but I knew Christ had me waiting for a reason. I knew He wanted to prepare my heart to trust Him with whatever happened and be prepared to receive it. Honestly, at times I fought with my mind not to think the worst, not to wonder if the doctor would perforate my ureter, or whether another complication would occur because let's face it, things happen. Just two weeks ago, they told me there was a 1% chance of there being complications with my epidural injection and I found myself in that 1%. Now I find myself wondering whether I'm in the 2% chance of possibly having a perforated ureter. I didn't know, but I knew the Lord did. This is why the Lord needed me to wait because he was giving me time to move from doubt to faith, not to have a complaining spirit but to understand that the waiting was by His design not the doctor's unexpected emergencies, and to use that time to worship and hear from Him. He needed to, once again, teach me about His sufficiency, His grace, His sovereign will. He needed me to be content in whatever state I was in or would be in later. For someone who is slightly controlling, this is very difficult. But He needed to show me how much more I need to make His word a living and breathing part of my life. I can't do this thing called life without Him.

Prior to today, the doctors told me I needed a cystoscopy because a kidney stone was lodged deep in my ureter with no other way out but laser surgery. After the six hour wait and my worrying, the doctors went in to find that they could not locate the kidney stone and therefore did not have to use the laser. You see, the Lord needed me to understand something more about Him. He said Andrea, they gave you a 1% and 2% chance but you forgot I'm in those percentages; Andrea, you forgot they gave you a prognosis of a kidney stone being lodged deep in your ureter, but you forgot, I have the final say. Nothing, absolutely nothing, happens on earth that I don't sanction in Heaven. It's not the doctors who have the final say, it's me. I need you to know that I will not fail you like others have. I need you to know that I won't leave you. I need you to know I won't lie to you. I need you to know you can depend on me. You can call me and I will answer. I got you girl, when will you receive that truth fully. I'm not the pain from your past, I am your joy, your healing, your peace, your deliverance, and undying love—past, present and future.

Scripture

"Be anxious for nothing but in everything by prayer and supplication and with thanksgiving, let your request be made know to God. And the peace of God, that surpasses all understanding, will guard your hearts and minds through Christ Jesus."

Philippians 4:6-7

CHAPTER FIFTY
Sleeping with the Enemy

As a school counselor, I have experienced hundreds of occasions where students have used their cell phones irresponsibly. Some kids cyberbully, while others take pictures, videos and text message in school, and post this information on the internet. This is disheartening for the school staff because many of the issues that occur in the evening, while the child is home, oftentimes spills into school for the staff to mediate. Parents become frustrated when we call home and inform them their child is involved in cyberbullying. They often ask what we are going to do to safeguard their child. And oftentimes it is their child that has initiated and continued to participate in cyberbullying, at all hours of the night, without their parents' knowledge.

What has been most astonishing is how uninformed parents are regarding their child's cell phone and computer use. And for some parents, they don't concern themselves because technology is so complex. One of the reasons cyberbullying is on the rise is because of pre-teens and teens electronic device accessibility in the evening without their parents' supervision. Unfortunately, cell phone or computer use does not just occur between the hours of 8:00 a.m. to 8:00 p.m. It occurs in the wee-hours of the night when you think your little darlings are snug-as-a-bug in the bed with their pillows, pets and stuffed teddy bears. Oh no, the typical bed companions of yesteryear are being replaced with your child's electronic devices.

Parents need to be aware of how after-hour cell phone usage can affect their children. Russell Rosenberg, PhD, Vice Chairman of the National Sleep Foundation, states 78% of teens, ages 12 and 13, and 86% of teens over the age of 14 are sleeping with their cell phones. When your teen's sleep pattern is disrupted, it has an effect on the way their body functions. Studies show low melatonin levels lead to an unhealthy lifestyle. We are prone to catching colds or the flu when we lack sleep. A lack of sleep can also make us more vulnerable to mental and/or mood problems, and physical health problems.

What astonishes me the most is some parent's lack of involvement surrounding their child's electronic devices? It is essential that parents safeguard their children from perpetrators, bullies, unwise website searches, and participating in defamatory communication which can affect their college and employment opportunities. Many parents have stated they trust their child or their child never lies to them. However, many parents are not communicating enough with their children about their day-to-day activities in and outside of school.

Whatever happened to the times when everyone sat at the dinner table together without the television or cell phones? Whatever happened to regular family meetings as a time to check in with one another? Whatever happened to quality family time? Our children may not be able to bend your ear due to your hectic schedules or life challenges but just know they are bending someone's ear. You want to make sure the advice that they are receiving is one that promotes your morals and beliefs.

It is not easy to ensure our teens get a good night's sleep. Parents, the more proactive you are will ensure your child gets sufficient rest and you will soon find out whether their electronic device is part of the problem. Proper monitoring will ensure your child is emotionally available to learn in school and in life.

Scripture

"These commandments that I give you today are to be upon your hearts. Impress them on your children. Talk about them when you sit at home and when you walk along the road, when you lie down and when you get up."

Deuteronomy 6:6-7

Thank You

Thank you for rejecting me. Thank you for judging me. Thank you for choosing not to forgive me. Thank you for being unreliable. Thank you for not hiring me when I was qualified. Thank you for making me do someone else's job and my own. Thank you for not wanting me as your own. Thank you for making me feel like I was unworthy. Thank you for making me feel like I was not good enough for you. Thank you for leaving me for another woman. Thank you for being unappreciative when I still decided to love you anyway. Thank you for not helping me when my heart cried out for relief. Thank you for reinforcing my insecurity by your lack of encouragement. Thank you for thinking less of me when I couldn't think more of myself. Thank you for calling me stupid and me believing it. Thank you for stabbing me in my back, dear friend. Thank you for not paying me back the money I loaned you when I didn't have enough to survive.

One might say why are you thanking these individuals for causing you pain and heartache? Why would you want to thank someone for not reimbursing you? Why would you want to thank someone for not supporting you in your time of need? During the time that I was going through these situations, the last thing on my mind was thanking these individuals. My flesh was hurting and I wanted them to hurt. I felt vulnerable, unimportant, abandoned and worthless. As a Christian, I can exercise looking at my pain two ways, as a victim or a victor. I can choose to fall prey to others actions towards me as defeat or I can choose to embrace the pain and allow it to work in my favor. One might ask, how can someone stabbing you in the back work out in your favor? How can someone who takes your last dime be a good thing?

James 1:2-4 says "Consider it a sheer gift, friends, when tests and challenges come at you from all sides. You know that under pressure, your faith-life is forced into the open and shows its true colors. So don't try to get out of anything prematurely. Let it do its work so you become mature and well-developed, not deficient in any way." James 1:2-4 reminds me of how gold is purified – through fire. When all the impurities are gone, you have 24-karat gold, which is the most valuable grade. So it is with us. One might believe all of my trials come to destroy me but they come to make me strong. The fire exposes my proclivity to enable others, my selfishness, my habits of relying on others instead of the Lord and how much faith I put in others to never fail me. The Lord is the only one who is the same yesterday, today and forever. He never changes. But people are fickle and change according to their emotions. If they are broke, they won't care if I'm on my last dime. But the real truth is, if I'm broke, why am I loaning anyone money? Because I care more about their perception of me than how I care for myself. That's why that occurred, to teach me something about myself, my Lord and other people. These lessons are gems for my life which only come to make me stronger. I am not defeated. I am victorious and even though it was painful, I thank God because I am better for it.

Scripture

"That is why, for Christ's sake, I delight in
weaknesses, in insults, in hardships,
in persecutions, in difficulties. For when
I am weak, then I am strong."

2 Corinthians 12:10

Hey Mommy

(everyone has a letter to write for healing)!

Hi mommy. I remember you. You were the woman I used to lay in bed with and play Barbie dolls. I remember you. You wouldn't let me leave the table until I ate my vegetables. I remember that. You made me feel safe as your daughter when I was bitten in the face by a dog. I remember you but I wish I had more to remember than my few memories. I remember when Aunt Betty died in 1968 and you took me and Tony to the funeral polar to view her body. I remember how you cried for your sister. I remember when we had an ice cream party and you smashed ice cream on my nose. Boy did Tony and I laugh. Grandmom (mom) was there too. I remember Shobby, your brother, being there too. I remember visiting you in the hospital. You were in a wheel chair and your face was full and round. I wondered why you had gained so much weight. I remember feeling like something wasn't quite right in the atmosphere but I was only seven years old, but I do remember. I remember a man waking me up (I thought it was daddy) and telling me you had died. I didn't really know what that meant but I knew I was supposed to cry, so I did. I remember a few days later when everyone left us at the house while they went to the funeral. Tony, Penny and I cried as we watched the family walk down the hill on Queen Lane. I remember the railroad tracks next to our house.

Mommy things didn't turn out so badly. I want to tell you some things. I was mad at you for leaving me. Even though I know it wasn't your fault. I know now it was God's permissive will and I'm getting okay with that. I am a school counselor and mental health counselor. I wish I had you so I would know what it feels like to have a mother. Then I wouldn't occasionally be jealous of other mother and daughter relationships. I realize not having you has given me a heart for little girls first and then the family as a whole. When I look at the children, I see me – the wounded and scared child. I wish I had more of me to go around as an adult because the need is so great. I need the children and their families to know that if I survived, you can too, and that I'm here to hold their hands. I want to walk them through their circumstances with all the power of the Lord. I want them to know and believe this – that they can make it.

Hey mommy, if I ever get rich, I'm going to purchase a large mansion for abused children and teens and then if I open a second facility, I will have one for the families. Yes, that's what I want to do. I can dream this for now and wait for its manifestation. You passed down your inner strength to me.

Mommy, I often wonder what life would have been like if you lived. I have only my imagination to use but I truly believe I would have been your main girl. We would have been best of friends. We would have gone shopping, like me and mom used to. It would have been the three of us. I wouldn't have felt out of place being at daddy's because we all would have been together. You know how kids always want their parents to be together even if the parents aren't meant to be together any longer. You would have spoiled my kids. Hey mommy, do you know Lauren, my baby girl, looks just like your picture at 19 years old. You both hold your mouth alike. Oh guess what mommy, do you know little Tony (he's in heaven with you now), he has a gap in his teeth like yours and so do I. That's our trademark. Someone once told me it was the trait of people who were born down south. We were born in Philadelphia.

Mommy, I just wanted to make my last entry about what our life would have been like if you had lived. Hey mommy, I remember once Tony tried to say something bad about you. Boy did I tear his head off. I told him you can't talk about my mother. She was perfect in my eyes and that's how it's going to remain. He knew I meant business and left me alone and didn't mention you in that way again. I think he was scared of me. Lol I won't let anyone disrespect you mommy. I got your back forever. Hey mommy, I still have your letters you wrote to Charles and Aunt Nietta. I can't always read them because it's still painful. Some might believe I'm over loosing you because I was so young. But I will never get over losing you.

Grandmom (mom) took good care of us mommy. I know you were watching over us and were proud. I often wondered what you thought when I did bad things. I knew you were watching right with Jesus. I just wanted to give you a shout out in my first book which I dedicate to you, grandmom (mom) and daddy. Hey mommy, daddy and I are close. I call him my stalker-daddy because he calls me every day. Hey mommy, he does love me. Really, he does. I'm his little Andy again and I'm grateful to have him. Hey mommy, Tony misses you too and still struggles a lot. We both were really messed up as kids, teens and adults but God is healing us. Hey mommy, you are my Proverbs 31 mommy. You feared the Lord and you are praised by me. Hey mommy, I love you and I miss you. Kiss grandmom (mom) for me. She was my rock for 44 years after your died. She did an excellent job. We were best friends. Hey mommy.

Scripture

Even though I walk through the valley of
the shadow of death, I will fear no evil,
for you are with me; your rod and your staff,
they comfort me.

Psalm 23:4

References

AZLyrics; retrieved November 2, 2013;
http://www.azlyrics.com/lyrics/steviewonder/lately.html

AZLyrics; retrieved November 2, 2013;
http://www.azlyrics.com/lyrics/temptations/justmyimaginationrunn ingawaywithme.html

A Time to Kill; retrieved November 2, 2013;
http://www.imdb.com/title/tt0117913/quotes

Asare, Lisa & Holder, Ariana. (2013). "No More Drama – Finding Favor In A Hateful Environment", Bethany Baptist Church.

Bahu, Erykah (1997). Song "Call Tyrone".

Black, Claudia. (2010). The Many Faces of Addiction. The Journal of Healing and Recovery; Understanding the Pain of Abandonment

Centers for Disease Control and Prevention. (2008). The Effects of Childhood Stress on Health Across the Lifespan.
http://www.cdc.gov/ncipc/pub-res/pdf/childhood_stress.pdf;
Retrieved March 29, 2014.

Evans, Bishop David G. (2013). A Person of Interest. Bethany Baptist Church

Gerlach, Peter (2013). MSW Break the Cycle; retrieved:
http://www.youtube.com/watch?v=ZEPAbxSnlFs&list=PLFDDB 7B5952B93B5B

Harvard Women's Health Watch (2007). Why it's hard to change unhealthy behavior—and why you should keep trying.
(*http://www.health.harvard.edu/newsweek/Why-its-hard-to-change-unhealthy-behavior.htm*; Retrieved October 31, 2013

Mandela, Nelson. GoodReads. *http://www.goodreads.com/quotes/144557-resentment-is-like-drinking-poison-and-then-hoping-it-will*

Meyers, Joyce. (Joyce Meyers, August 1, 2013, tv message, at 1:53).

Meyers, Joyce (1987). The Everyday Life Bible (Amplified Version)

Meyers, Joyce. *http://www.youtube.com/watch?v=3Kx1C3h4DUs*)

Oprah, Why Do People Hoard; *http://www.oprah.com/home/Why-People-Become-Compulsive-Hoarders*. Retrieved November 11, 2013

Pandora's Closet, Older People Surviving Child Sexual Abuse, 2010 Pandora's Aquarium By: Louise; retrieved November 30, 2013.

Rosenberg, Russell, PhD; Annual Sleep in America Poll Exploring Connections with Communications Technology Use and Sleep; March 7, 2011

Simpson, Nicole B. (2010). Dare 2 Dream. Harvest Wealth Media Group; 1st Edition

Statistics (2013). The Fatherless Generation; *http://thefatherlessgeneration.wordpress.com/statistics*; retrieved November 1, 2013

Thoele, Sue P. (2001). The Courage to be Yourself. Conari Press

Turner, Stephen P. Conflict in Organizations: Practical solutions any manager can use; University of South Florida; 1983.

Vanzant, Iyanla, (2013) Retrieved Facebook on November 1, 2013.

Williams, Christopher (1989). Song "Promises Promises".

Winfrey, Opray. SuperSoulSunday. Oprah and Michael Singer: The Untethered Soul; Season 3, Episode 322, Aired on 8/5/12

About The Author

Andrea Bing Brown is the Founder and CEO of 21st Century Parenting, an anti-cyberbullying business. Andrea is a school counselor and a mental health counselor. Andrea believes what makes her role as a school counselor unique is her experience as a mental health counselor. She understands the intricacies involved in intergenerational style of relating which form our intrapersonal styles which affects our relationships with others. Once you understand how this style is formed, you can take strategic steps towards reinventing yourself to live a healthier and more productive life.

Andrea Bing-Brown has a passion for inspiring people to strive to their fullest potential despite their circumstances. She grew up with an impoverished mindset which affected her self-perception which controller her choices. Now she is a woman who decides daily to embrace her God-given beauty and confidence within. THAT'S FREEDOM!

Andrea conducts parent and teenage workshops on cyberbullying and woman's workshops on self-awareness.

Andrea lives in New Jersey and has four adult children and seven grandchildren. Andrea attends Bethany Baptist Church in Lindenwold, NJ where Bishop David G. Evans is the pastor.

For additional copies of Kaleidoscope, please contact:

Andrea Bing Brown
609-792-5504
Email: *kaleidoscope609@comcast.net*

Favorite scripture

"As iron sharpens iron, so a man sharpens the countenance of a friend."

Proverbs 27:17

Favorite quotes

"The moment you settle for less than what you deserve, is the moment you get less than what you settled for."

Maureen Dowd